Divine Intervention

Brenda Lee Birch

First Edition – September 2023
ISBN 978-1-7380268-0-7
ISBN E-Book 978-1-7380268-14

Publishing Services by Peony Cottage Publishing

Bible Quotations from New International Version and Revised Standard Version

Cover Design by Wendy Ballantyne

Acknowledgements

When I wrote my stories and plays as a young child, it was a solo adventure.

When you write a book for publication, it becomes a group adventure.

I want to thank those who joined me on this adventure.

My family, who has been with me the longest—Doug, Zachary, and Nathaniel—without whom these stories could not have been written.

My writers' group—Tandy, Alida, and Kathleen—who have all been so encouraging.

Tom, who tirelessly formatted, always with patience and good humour.

Wendy, who gave generously in designing the cover for this book.

Tandy, who was my publishing mentor and encourager.

My Readers who generously gave their time and helpful comments.

God bless each one.

What People are Saying about Divine Intervention

For many, the concept of God is a vague fuzzy world that seems remote from day to day. Many acknowledge that God is the creator of the universe, but does He really involve himself in the lives of people? The remarkable lives of Doug and Brenda Birch fly in the face of such thinking.

Brenda skillfully writes a series of vignettes of their life experiences demonstrating that He delights in responding to the wants and needs of people of faith. It is not that God jumps in occasionally but is involved moment by moment.

Readers who know God, will be greatly encouraged to live more intimately with God. Those who do not value God, will be hard pressed to explain the long chain of "coincidences"! Any reader will receive inspiration from this good "read"!

~ James Stenstrom

Chance? Coincidence? Luck?

Those are the words the world might use for the life stories Brenda shares in this book. They are the true stories of her life and take a magnificent picture of her life.

God does not use those words either, but He does use our neighbours, and the people we meet on the road. Brenda portrays these vignettes through the eyes of her faith in our Almighty God. Enjoy the stories and let them help you to open your eyes to God's work in your life.

~Alida Van Polanen

This book had a beautiful testimony that the good and faithful God of the Old and New Testament is deeply interested in hearing and answering the prayers of today. A book that will surely bring hope and comfort to an anxious world.

~ Natalie Walter

I'm not much of a reader these days, audio books are what works best for me, but I found this book to be an easy read. The short stories in it captivated me and kept me wanting to know what the next story was about. As a believer I found these stories got me thinking long after I finished reading, to think about my own trust and faithfulness in God.

I found the common thread in these stories to be uncomplicated trust and prayer. These two things allowed for moving forward.

To be honest it was inspiring to see someone's life, full of trials, and tribulations, always move to positive outcomes, despite the unknown.

If you are going through a tough moment, or season, I highly recommend this book to remind you we aren't alone in tough times.

~ Nayely Sedlacek

About the Author

Brenda was born in Flin Flon Manitoba and lived her entire childhood on the Canadian Prairies.

Brenda and her husband are delighted to be living near their granddaughters, and other family members.

Family, faith and friends are what bring the most joy to Brenda.

She also enjoys reading, writing, gardening, and acting.

Brenda has written many skits and plays, stories, meditations and devotionals and some poetry.

Her focus, in her life and in her writing, is to proclaim Christ and to bring hope to others.

Introduction

Over the years as I have shared some of my stories in public readings or with the members of my Writing Group, there have been some that clearly touched hearts. As a result of this I have often thought of them as my favorite stories.

Although this book has been written over several years it was not until this book was progressing thru the Publishing phase that I realized which story had impacted my life the most. This story's outcome built the foundation of my relationship with God.

I learned that God listened, and He answered. This was etched on my heart and soul at a very young age, and I have had many more occasions to reinforce these truths. Turn the page to the Table of Contents, this story is the first one listed.

If you know God as your Saviour, I rejoice with you. If you do not know Him, my prayer is that you will meet Him in the pages of this book.

Blessings to all my readers Brenda Lee Birch

Contents

The Little Red Book

I have known from a very young age that God answers prayer. Although I am not certain when the story that I am going to share with you happened. I can pinpoint it as having occurred when I was about four or five years old.

Our family was living in the green and yellow house in Winnipeg, with the large tree in the front yard, surrounded by a black iron fence with a gate that I loved to swing on to while away the long summer days.

On one such day, a gentleman with a briefcase stopped and asked if my mother was home. I said yes and ran ahead of the gentleman to open the front door. I excitedly called my mom to let her know that we had a visitor.

It turned out that our visitor wanted to sell something to my mother. We lived in a Jewish neighborhood, and my mother could hold her own with the other women on the block, sending unwanted salesmen who arrived at our door off with a flea in their ear!

But wonder of wonders, this salesman left our house with an order for a book of Bible stories.

I was sure that Christmas and my birthday and Easter must have all happened at once on that very afternoon, I was so excited. A book was going to come to our house for my two sisters and me. Our very own book.

Every day when the postman arrived at our door, I would run to see if he had brought our book to us. Each day my shoulders would slump with disappointment when there was no sign of the book.

Time passed. Days soon became weeks, and the weeks turned into months. Still no book.

Finally, my mother had enough of my pestering and told me that the salesman was supposed to deliver the book to us. So, there was no point running to the door and pestering the postman.

I pondered this information and then acted. I had a faithful Sunday School teacher who prayed with us each Sunday morning, and she told us that God was a good listener and would answer our prayers.

I knelt beside my bed and explained the problem to God. I reminded him what had happened and what was supposed to happen and asked him to please send us the little red book. "Please!" I entreated him with all my heart.

Surprisingly, the book did not arrive the next day—or the one after either. But I still prayed because I believed God could make it happen.

And He did! The little red book was delivered by the nice salesman. He probably wasn't used to such a reception. Three little girls jumped up and down with excitement and squeals, our mom vainly trying to bring some order and quiet.

Of course, as soon as the salesman left, we demanded that mom read to us.

For many years, each evening Mom would read us a story from that precious little red book before we went to bed. The book had many bent and loose pages as the years moved on, but we never tired of hearing the stories.

God answered my prayers, and I never forgot that. The certainty was locked into my mind and my heart.

Many years later, my sisters and I were visiting our mom while she was in Care. We were waiting in the lobby while the nurses were finishing her morning routine. I glanced over at the bookcase beside the fireplace. There were some different books on the bottom shelf. My eyes ran over the titles. Suddenly, I stopped.

It couldn't be! A copy of our little red book! I grabbed it and called my sisters' attention to what I had found. We sat down and flipped through the pages. It was so amazing to see the little red book again, although this copy was in much better shape. We eagerly searched for our favourite stories. They were all there.

Too soon we were interrupted. We asked permission to take it to show our mom. It was such a blessing remembering Mom reading the stories to us. I briefly thought about offering to donate other books or a cash donation for the book itself but decided that I would not. Perhaps the book would bless some children who had to wait in the lobby.

I never saw that book again. I checked all the shelves several times, but it was gone! Was I disappointed? No, I wasn't. Just as God had his perfect timing for the book's arrival when we were small children, the book's arrival the second time was perfect as well.

A Small Blue Car

My husband was studying at Bible College, and I was working with special needs children at Sunnyside Rehab Hospital in Vancouver.

One Saturday morning, we were going out for groceries, and we were in a car accident. Our car was the third car in a four-car pileup. So, our car resembled an accordion, squished at both ends. Remarkably, all four doors still opened, but it was a write-off. My neck was injured. So, I left the hospital in a neck brace.

We needed a replacement car, as I worked quite a distance from our home. A friend lent us a car until we settled our claim with our insurance. We found a little blue Mazda, but with no cash on hand, we had to leave the car behind. Then we got the bad news. Our insurance wouldn't cover the accident.

After my Speech and Language class, my teacher, who was also a good friend, asked how our car search was going. I explained our predicament but told her that we had confidence that God would provide a car for us.

She smiled at me and said, "I have a proposal for you and Doug."

Mrs. Stevens offered to give us the money to purchase the Mazda. She didn't want us to pay her back. Instead, she asked us to help another person at some point in the future who was in a similar predicament. Many years previously, Mrs. Stevens had received the same proposal when she needed help, the same admonition to pay it forward.

As I watched her write the cheque, I could hardly breathe, in wonder at the way God had answered our prayer and in wonder that we would, one day, have the privilege to be His instrument to help someone else.

We drove that small blue car for several years and never had any mechanical problems. It truly was a blessed car. Long after it was gone, we were able to help a friend who needed a car for their family and couldn't afford to buy one. It was a delight and a blessing to see the wonder on their faces as they joined this amazing plan of God.

I am not sure even today when I felt the most wonder and blessing. Was it when I sat and watched a cheque being written for me or when I was the one who was able to bless my friend by giving her the gift of a much-needed car? I may never be able to answer this question, but, either way, all these circumstances were God's plan for each of us, both the blessed and the conduit of blessings.

The golden cord that strung all of us together was woven by God to bring good to His children.

"We know that in everything God works for good with those who love him, who are called according to his purpose" (Romans 8:28 RSV).

All These Things

My husband and I were married only a year when the battle began. It was in my husband's heart and was unspoken. Even though he did not share the nature of the battle, I was aware that he was struggling and that the struggle was with the Lord.

In the meantime, my husband decided to start working towards his Certified General Accounting degree. He studied and attended night classes while maintaining his position with the Calgary Public School Board. We dreamed dreams of prospering and building a home and having a family.

Year Two of our marriage began with a very serious conversation. "Honey," my husband began, "I can't fight with the Lord any longer. I want to finish my accounting degree and be able to give you the life we have been dreaming about. The Lord wants me to go to Bible College."

It was a good thing that the Holy Spirit had been whispering in my ear, "Be prepared. Be ready." I knew that something was going to change but really wasn't thinking of such an about face. We did a 360-degree turn around. It kind of made us dizzy since it happened so fast.

We maintained our jobs as Doug applied for admission to Bible College. We gave up our apartment and put our furniture in storage in Doug's parents' basement. We looked for people we knew who were planning holidays, and we offered to stay in their homes and cut lawns and do general maintenance chores and provide security. We needed to save some money for college fees and living expenses until we were moved to British Columbia and I was able to find a job.

Several people in our church and some others from where Doug worked agreed to have us housesit their homes, but there were many who questioned our decisions. They were concerned that we were taking a lot of financial risks—with no backup plans.

We were delighted to share the scriptures that God had shown us as we started this journey of faith and obedience.

"But if God so clothes the grass of the field, which today is alive and tomorrow is thrown into the oven, will he not much more clothe you, O men of little faith. Therefore, do not be anxious, saying 'What shall we eat?' or 'What shall we drink?' or 'What shall we wear?' For the Gentiles seek all these things; and your heavenly Father knows that you need them all. But seek first his kingdom and his righteousness and all these things shall be yours as well" (Matthew 6:30-33).

Just a week before we left, my father-in-law came to me. "Honey, do you have enough money? Doug's not saying."

I smiled at him and said that we had enough money for one month's living expenses and could pay for one semester of school. I smiled with absolute confidence. This was a wondrous amount and that we had no worries.

Dad patted my shoulder and turned away saying, "Okay." He was possibly not as confident as we were.

We packed our books and clothes and a few household items and drove off happy and confident because we believed God when He said, "…and all these things shall be yours as well."

Our youth pastor's parents were visiting their son at our church when our church gave us a wonderful sendoff potluck supper. After supper was over, they introduced themselves to us and offered us a place to stay in Vancouver until we found a job and a home.

One week after we arrived in Vancouver, we had an apartment and a job. One day after we moved in, we had a bed, a couch that was missing a few legs, a table, and two chairs. We used some of Doug's thick theology books to replace those missing legs on the couch. We felt that God had given us a wondrous home and job.

Over the next four years, God continued make sure we had "all these things." The best was when we would receive a cheque in the mail from someone in our church back home and we didn't know what it was for. We had no bill that needed to be paid. So, we put the cheque back in the envelope, tucked it away, and waited. Sure enough, before too long, something was needed—an oil change, gas for the car, groceries—and the cheque that we had already received was the exact amount needed.

And as each new semester of school arrived, so did the money to pay the fees. We finished four years of school with no debt. God indeed had provided "all things," as He had promised.

When we finished school, we thought that was the end, but it turned out to be only the beginning. God had many more plans for us and continued to provide repeatedly.

He is a good, good Father.

All Packed

We were all packed. The moving truck was coming at 5:00 Friday evening to start loading and would return in the morning to finish.

The truck and several men arrived, and I started directing which rooms I wanted to be loaded that evening.

We had purchased a small character home in Winnipeg and were looking forward to getting settled and take up our responsibilities at the new church we had been called to pastor.

Just as the men started to carry out furniture, the phone rang. It was our realtor from Winnipeg.

"Brenda, I have some bad news. The deal we had on the little house has collapsed. The family has changed their mind."

I was shocked. We had some decisions to make, and they had to be made quickly. We were up against a strict deadline, as the new owners of our current home had already given us two extensions for vacating, and they were going to move in as soon as we were out the following day.

The realtor had an option for us. "Do you remember the townhouse that I showed you?" she asked.

"Only the orange shag carpet and the dark kitchen," I replied.

"Would you consider making an offer on the townhouse? It is empty."

"I guess so. There don't seem to be any other options."

"It is a CHMC house. So, I will be at the door early in the morning and talk to the agent. I will make sure that you can move in tomorrow. I will call you in the morning as soon as I have an answer," the realtor assured me.

I gave her our friend's phone number, as we were going to their house for supper and a birthday celebration. The realtor was going to come out to Portage La Prairie later in the evening so we could sign the new Offer to Purchase.

"One more thing, Brenda. The townhouse costs more. So, we will need another $300 for the downpayment."

I reminded her that we had no money to cover that.

"We won't worry about that right now. We will deal with that tonight" was her parting comment.

By the time the phone call was finished, I realized that the truck loading had come to a halt and all the men who had come to load the truck were standing around me.

"What do we do now?" one of them asked.

"Keep loading. We have to be out of this place by noon tomorrow," my husband responded.

We had a time of prayer before the loading resumed.

Later that night, we recounted the events of the afternoon to our friends as we ate supper. We gathered around the table for a time of prayer, asking God to work things out for a place to live. My husband assured me that God wouldn't give us a job without providing a home for us. He knew what we needed.

At 9:00 the call came from the realtor that she was in town. We gave her directions to our home, and leaving our son to play with his friend, we returned to our house to meet with her. The realtor had travelled with her business partner and her partner's husband. We didn't blame her. It was a typical January night in Manitoba, dark and icy with blowing snow. We reviewed the details of the offer and signed the document.

"I mentioned that this offer required an additional $300 be attached to it." Saying this, our realtor reached into her briefcase and withdrew three $100 bills and placed them on the table. "Now we have everything we need," she stated. "And this is a gift, not a loan. You have not been treated right."

The next morning, the men returned and continued to load the truck. The morning seemed to move slowly, everybody glancing at the phone each time they passed it. When it finally rang, everybody stopped what they were doing. I lifted the receiver.

"Brenda, I have just finished meeting with the CMHC agent. We have had a long conversation." There was a pause. "I have called you now that we have a decision." There was another pause. "You have a house!"

The last phrase was spoken so loudly that everyone in the house heard it. Cheers and clapping filled the room.

"Thank you. That is such good news! Thank you for all that you have done for us! We are so grateful!"

We continued our conversation, making arrangements to meet at the church where we were going to be pastoring. Not only did I not remember much about the house that we had just bought, but neither my husband nor I had any idea where it was located.

When the last box found its home on the truck and the last room was swept, we all went to a friend's home for a fabulous homecooked dinner. It was a great time of testimony to and gratitude for God's provision. We were all packed and ready for our new adventure.

Bible College

We had been married for less than two years when my husband felt God was calling him to go to Bible College. It was exciting but daunting.

The first obstacle was his educational background. He had not completed high school. This was not because of a lack of ability or unwillingness but because of a huge upheaval and changes in the school system in the province in which he was residing the summer he was between grades 11 and 12. They no longer had a program for him.

His parents sent him to another province, where they were greeted with the news that he would be required to start in grade 9 in order to meet the educational requirements for high school graduation in that province.

After searching for options and praying, they found out that because of his age, he was eligible to apply for Business College. He completed the course and was able to find a good job.

Our second challenge was that we did not have the financial resources to leave our jobs.

(Please see the story "All These Things" to see how God divinely interceded on our behalf in this challenge.)

Doug applied to Northwest Baptist College and Seminary. At the bottom of his application, he noted that he was only eligible for the one-year certificate course. With fear and trembling, he asked the registrar to consider allowing him entrance to the three-year Licentiate of Theology program. Then we sent the application away and started preparing to go to Bible College. We knew we were going to attend, just not for how long.

We prayed and watched the mailbox anxiously for the answer. We had wonderful encouragement and prayer support from family and friends. Finally, the envelope appeared in our mailbox, and we excitedly tore it open.

Have you ever asked God for something and then been overwhelmed when He gave you above and beyond what you could imagine?

When we read the acceptance letter, we almost stopped breathing. God had divinely intervened in our life. We did not have a big enough dream, and He was showing us that He had divinely intervened so that we could be prepared for His purposes and plans for our life! Doug had been accepted for the three-year Licentiate of Theology program, but they recommended that he enter the four-year Bachelor of Theology program!

This was the beginning of our adventure, experiencing God's love, care, protection, provision, and intervention. He is a mighty God!

Practicing the Presence of Christ

We moved in the month of January amid a Manitoba snowstorm. The house was freezing as the door had to be left open for the men to move in boxes and furniture.

My husband was taking up responsibilities as pastor of a new congregation, and our five-year-old son was starting in a new school for kindergarten as well as a new teacher for his piano lessons. I was unpacking and recreating our home and trying to find the nearest grocery stores and a family doctor. We would leave meeting new neighbors for warmer days. The days flew by, and we all settled in comfortably, getting to know members of our congregation.

We had a community skating rink in the open green spaces in front of our home. Our son, Zachary, would get off the school bus at lunchtime, walk through the back door of the house, and continue to the front door, exchanging his boots for skates. It was great fun watching him skate with neighbor children from my living room window.

A few months after our arrival in Winnipeg, we found out that I was expecting a baby. This was an occasion for great joy mixed with some trepidation. I had lost two babies already and had very complicated pregnancies. Soon, I was on total bedrest and very ill with morning sickness, which lasted twenty-four hours a day for about five months. After five months, I had toxemia and threw up blood.

I lay on the couch watching Zachary skate. Then he would eat the lunch that my husband had prepared for him before leaving the house in the morning. Two afternoons a week, a lady from the congregation would come and pick up Zachary for the afternoon to play with her children.

The worst part of the pregnancy were the massive headaches I had. I couldn't read, listen to the radio, or even look at a magazine. It was too painful. But the Lord had plans for me even during this precarious pregnancy while I was lying on my bed.

Two momentous events occurred during the months of my enforced inactivity. I found that I could pray without any increase in pain. During the months on my bed, I started to pray for our family and members of our congregation. It doesn't sound like much, but I talked to God a lot. I had many long conversations with Him. I found the time spent with Him built an increased intimacy and deepening relationship with Him.

My bedroom became my prayer closet. It was quiet, warm, and interruption free as we met each morning. His presence surrounded me like a warm blanket, and I poured out my thoughts and fears. I was never lonely during those months because I felt His presence surrounding me. My fears about pregnancy were calmed. I stopped having nightmares about miscarriages and stillborn babies.

The second momentous event came out of my constant search for what God was calling me to do for Him, to serve Him. Each day part of our conversations included this subject at some point. After many weeks something happened. I sensed that I needed to open my Bible. My spirit was being urged to do this despite the pain that this simple action had caused in the past. As I talked to God, the urge became stronger and stronger.

I reached for my Bible and put it on my lap. I pondered for some time. I couldn't read the entire Bible. What was the alternative?

I pondered for a while, then decided to pray. "Lord I am going to open my Bible, and I believe that when I do this, You will direct my eyes to Your purpose for my life in serving You."

I picked up my Bible and opened it. It opened to Jeremiah 30. My eyes fell on verse 2, "This is what the Lord, the God of Israel says: 'Write in a book all the words I have spoken to you.'"

I was stunned. I had been writing skits and stories since I was eight years old. He wanted me to write a book! I had always felt that I didn't have the attention span to write a book, never mind enough words to fill one.

I read the last phrase again. My breathing slowed down. He was going to speak the works to me that I was to write. I smiled. "Okay, that makes it possible. I don't have to think up all the words by myself."

My second son was born in the fall of that year, healthy and strong. I will always remember those precious months of lying in my bed. Only God and I in close communion. Only one verse, but it set the direction of my life.

So, now I am coming close to finishing my first book and have enough words for possibly three or more additional books. God does everything in abundance. He only asks that I listen and obey.

The Spiritual Stove

My husband and I were pastoring a church in Manitoba. We were renting a home, as the church did not have a parsonage. The house was large and filled with light, and we had a large backyard for our son to play in. Our landlady was gracious, and we felt richly blessed in the church and in our community.

I think we had lived in this home for about a year when the landlady called one afternoon and asked if she could drop in later that evening. We were curious but not concerned. When she arrived, she appeared nervous. The first thought was that she was going to tell us that she had decided to sell the house. The house had been on the market when we were looking for a home to rent the previous year. She had been unable to find a purchaser so had agreed to take it off the market and rent it to us.

It took her some time, but eventually, she explained that her daughter was moving into a home of her own and that the daughter needed a stove. It took us a few minutes, but we realized that our landlady wished to help her daughter out by giving her the stove that was in our kitchen. She said she would allow us some time to replace the stove but made it clear that it would be a limited time.

The next morning, we began our search. We started with the second-hand furniture stores and the classified ads. We found stoves that were too big, too old, or that brought to mind some of the scary stoves of our student days.

Eventually, we decided to drive into the city and look at new stoves even though we weren't sure how we would manage the monthly payments. We found the perfect stove. I would like to say that we were very spiritually minded at this point and laid hands on the stove and claimed it in the Lord's name. The truth is that I was so enamored by this object of shiny porcelain and steel that I couldn't get my hands off it long enough to have any sane thoughts.

When my husband was finally able to catch my attention, he gently reminded me of the state of our finances. Ah, the refreshing cold splash of reality! I looked longingly over my shoulder as we left the store.

Arriving home late that evening, the red light on our answering machine was blinking. The landlady was arriving the following morning to take the stove out of our kitchen. We managed with a frying pan, a camp stove, and a BBQ out under the carport.

After supper a few days later, my husband walked over to the empty space previously occupied by a stove and turned to me. "We need to thank the Lord for our spiritual stove," he informed me.

"What spiritual stove?" I asked.

"The one right here," he replied, indicating the empty space.

"Oh, okay," I reluctantly agreed, while I tried to figure out what had happened to my normally sane down-to-earth husband.

My husband then went on to explain that while we thanked the Lord for the spiritual stove, he was confident that it would be replaced by a real stove. He didn't know how or when, but my husband was confident that God had a plan and time and it would be perfect.

Every mealtime we would thank God for our spiritual stove, and soon it became a time of thankfulness and excitement as we waited to see how and when the spiritual stove would be replaced by a physical stove. Our church was interested in how this was going to work out, and many were praying alongside us.

After breakfast one morning, a friend called and asked if we could get together for coffee that evening. We always enjoyed their company, and they had a little girl close in age to our son. So, we were looking forward to the visit.

Once the coffee was served and the kids were playing, the conversation turned to our spiritual stove and the wait for its replacement. Then they told us about their breakfast earlier that morning. After completing their devotions, they had a time of prayer. As they opened their eyes, they looked at each other across the table and spoke the same words at the same time, "Let's give Doug and Brenda the money for the stove."

We were stunned. It was to be a loan with no payment structure. We were to pay it back to them however and whenever it was convenient for us. The timing and the method, monthly or all at once, was our choice.

The next few days were exciting, as we borrowed a truck (the gas was provided by another parishioner) to drive to the city.

The stove that we had so desired was still available. That evening, there was a crowd at our door when we arrived home. They were waiting to see the stove that God had provided. As the stove was installed, there was much praise and delight in our Lord.

Three months after our physical stove arrived, our friends who had so generously provided the money, were laid off from their job.

"Doug, they gave us the money for the stove. They could really use that money right now. We must return their gift."

A glance at our bank balance told us that there was only a tiny portion of the amount we needed. We went to prayer, confident that our God could fill up our bank account with the amount needed. Within a few days, all the money was in the bank. It's true! It really happened! We were so excited!

We called our friends and invited them over for tea that evening. Once tea was served and the kids were playing, conversation turned to our friends' employment prospects. They felt that something would turn up but that it could take some time, as we lived in a small rural community.

By this time, we were bursting. With big smiles, we put the cash in our friends' hands. It was their turn to be stunned!

"Are you sure?" they questioned.

"Absolutely! Take the money and run!" we advised with a laugh.

As we recounted how the Lord had deposited the money into our bank account, once again, all of us were able to rejoice in the amazing God we all loved and served.

There is an old hymn whose chorus goes like this:

> God will take care of you,
> In every way, thru every day,
> God will take care of you,
> He will take care of you.

He only asks that you trust Him, for He is faithful. God loves to pour His blessings on His children. He promises that when we call on Him, He will answer.

"Call to me and I will answer you and tell you great and unsearchable things you do not know" (Jeremiah 33:3 NIV).

Our friends listened to the direction of the Holy Spirit during their devotions that morning. They were able to bless us as God used them as His answer to our petition for a stove. We had an opportunity to ask God for help so that we in turn could help our friends. God answered our prayers in a way that only He could, allowing us to be His instrument to bring a blessing to our friends.

The Calling

I was pregnant. In a bad way. Not for the first time. I was on total bed rest, throwing up constantly, day after day. Well past the first trimester. I had massive headaches. The doctor called them muscle spasms, but it didn't matter what they were called. My head was held in a tight grip twenty-four hours a day.

I could not read, watch TV, or listen to the radio. Turning a page of a magazine hurt my head. My five-year-old son played beside my bed each afternoon, content to be in my company after a busy morning in kindergarten.

Still, looking at the blank wall at the foot of my bed got old quickly. We had moved to a new city where my husband took up the position of pastor of a small church. He would often call me with a request for prayer. He was facing some difficult situations and he needed wisdom.

I discovered that I could pray without an increase of nausea or muscle spasms. This discovery was a pivotal point in my life, I became a prayer warrior, long before the term was used. I spent hours praying each morning, often for people who I only knew by name.

I eagerly looked forward to my time in His presence. I was praying for others, no longer focused on myself. God became my closest friend, surrounding me with peace and the warmth of His love.

As my time of prayer ended each day and the awareness of my pain and discomfort returned, I realized that He was providing me with the strength I needed to handle my condition with grace.

One morning during my prayer time, the Holy Spirit led my thoughts to something I had been pondering for a long time.

"Lord, I have been enjoying our time so much." Then I blurted out, "What do you want me to do? What is my gift?"

I felt the Holy Spirit nudging my thoughts towards the Bible lying on my nightstand.

"Not a good idea," I thought. I had not read my Bible since the onset of my pregnancy because of the muscle spasms.

I lay there for a while. It was very quiet. Nothing happened. Reluctantly, I reached for my Bible, while objecting, "You know, Lord, that this is a big book. I'm not sure where to start."

The quiet continued. Finally, I opened the Bible. I was hesitant to read because that would cause the pain from the muscle spasms to increase.

"You know that I can only read for a few seconds at the most," I reminded Him.

Looking down at my Bible I saw that I was in the book of Jeremiah. My eyes fell on Jeremiah 30:2, "This is what the Lord, the God of Israel, says, 'Write in a book all the words I have spoken to you.'"

Pivot! In that one verse, God had given me a direct command and answered my worry about having enough words to write a whole book. He would give me the words to say! I didn't have to worry about that ever again. I closed my Bible with a big smile, confident I had heard His voice that morning.

Pivot!

They That Wait on The Lord

It was the first time my husband delivered a sermon from a barstool.

Earlier in the week, he had offered to help a lady move some things into her new home. She had recently returned to the city and was newly widowed. He hauled many items up several flights of stairs, but it was the microwave that was his undoing. It was big and awkward and very heavy.

By Sunday morning, he could hardly walk and could stand for only a limited time. He told one of the elders that he didn't think he would be able to deliver the sermon without sitting. So, he did it sitting on a barstool.

Later that day, he was admitted to the hospital and put into traction. Over the next few days, several specialists were called in for consultations. They all agreed on one thing: he needed complicated surgery.

As I was praying one night after I had put our two little ones to bed, I called out to the Lord in my distress. We had been told that afternoon that if Doug had the surgery, he would not walk again. As the doctors had all declined to do the surgery because of the risk factors, we were in a quandary. They also weren't sure if, when he was released from traction, he would be able to walk either.

I opened my Bible blindly through my tears. The Bible had fallen open to *"...but they who wait for the Lord shall renew their strength, they shall mount up with wings like eagles, they shall run and not be weary, they shall walk and not faint" (Isaiah 40:31).*

That verse seared itself upon my heart and mind. I typed it on a piece of paper and took it to the hospital the next morning. As my husband and I rejoiced over the verse and the promises it contained, we decided that I should tape it on the wall above Doug's bed.

Each visitor and each hospital staff could not help but notice it as they came into my husband's hospital room over the next few days. It generated many opportunities for conversation, questions, and sharing about the great God who could fulfill the promises in this verse. I was so excited and filled with hope and joy that I never stopped to consider the next step. But my husband did.

I entered his room one hot Winnipeg summer afternoon. I stopped in the doorway in shock. All the traction apparatus was gone. Doug was sitting up in his bed, quietly waiting for my reaction.

He motioned to the chair beside his bed. He took my hands in his and asked me a question, "Do you really believe the promises in the verse you brought me?" he asked.

"Of course," I replied.

"Good. We have claimed these promises, but now it is time to act on them. I told the doctor to remove the traction and also talked to a physiotherapist before you came. After some persuasion and conversation, it was agreed that I could start gentle exercises but that I would have to wear a back brace.

They said I would probably still end up in a wheelchair, but we know differently. You can't run in a chair."

Doug was fitted for a back brace, discharged from the hospital soon after, and continued daily exercises with the physiotherapist at the hospital.

Two months later, we attended our denominations annual conference. As we entered the building, we were surrounded by many people who had been praying for us. They were astounded that Doug was walking and many asked how he was feeling. His reply: "Great! Thank you."

As Doug moved through the groups that were gathered around us, several people turned to me and asked, "How is he really?"

I smiled. "Great. He only wears the brace occasionally, when he is tired. And he has managed to take a few motorcycle rides in the last week. He says that was the best therapy he could have, being able to ride his motorcycle again."

Isaiah 40:31 has remained in my heart and mind for these many years. It is one of the many verses God has given us and shown that He is a God who keeps His promises. He will neve leave us or forsake us.

Scripture is rich with promises for His children. They are freely given and always lovingly bestowed.

Bountiful Provision

My husband had recently resigned as the pastor of a city church. We had a very limited income, as my husband had applied to Graduate School on a part-time basis and was working two days a week for a friend. All of these changes occurred within a short space of time. So, we were not prepared financially.

Two weeks before my husband's classes were to begin, he went to the school campus to register. After standing in lines for the better part of the morning, he had selected the courses that he needed to take. He was in the last line where he would find out the cost of his courses.

Finally, his turn came. Handing in his paper listing course names and class times, he waited while the information was entered into the computer. The lady at the desk smiled and named the amount due for fees. My husband smiled at the lady and informed her that he did not have any money that he could give her that day. She asked him when he would have the money. He told her that he would have the money on the first day of class.

"Jehovah Jirah, the Lord provides!" he reminded her with a smile.

"Due before you go to your first class," she told him firmly.

The school fees arrived from several different sources over the next two weeks. Doug received a letter in the mail paying him for a preaching engagement that he had undertaken so long ago that we had forgotten about it and that we hadn't been paid. I found some money when cleaning out drawers that I had stashed away at some point. Sometimes housework is more rewarding than others. More than once, we were handed envelopes privately that contained cash. The Lord is very creative, and it was exciting when Doug arrived for his first day of classes, fees paid in full.

That was the first year that we had not been able to put in a garden. Each summer for several years, we had been given a huge plot on one of our church member's acreage. We had filled our old 25 cubic foot freezer with the vegetables that we'd harvested from the garden. This harvest was after our family, as well as many of our neighbors, had feasted on fresh-from-the-garden produce all summer.

This year of school and part-time work was going to be difficult with an almost empty freezer. The Lord, however, has vast resources and plans that we cannot imagine.

"'For my thoughts are not your thoughts, neither are your ways my ways,' declares the Lord. 'As the heavens are higher than the earth, so are my ways higher than your ways and my thoughts than your thoughts'" (Isaiah 55:8-9 NIV).

A member of our church had a death in his family that fall. The man and his wife had owned and operated a grocery store in a nearby community. The widow did not intend to continue with the store by herself. She called the church member and asked if he knew of anyone who wanted to buy canned goods at wholesale prices. We scraped together some cash and Doug returned home with several boxes of canned goods.

As I was trying to find room in my recently emptied cupboards and pantry, my son commented, "Mom, God sure filled our cupboards!"

Such a bountiful provision from an amazing God! We had enough food to feed our family and many guests over the winter and into the spring.

(Please see the story "Making Dad a Grad" to see how God continued to divinely intervene for our family so that my husband could work on his Master's degree fulltime.)

No White Crosses for Us

In Montana scattered along Highway 2 are small white crosses. These crosses are placed where there have been traffic fatalities. My husband, Doug, and I and our two sons were on holiday. We were travelling with our friends Allan and Ellen and their two children. We had entered Montana just a few hours earlier.

Leaving Winnipeg four days earlier, we had all been camping and enjoying the sights of North Dakota. It had rained hard almost every day, but by the time we were ready to set up camp, the sun was shining brightly. While the adults were setting up camp and preparing dinner, the kids were swimming and playing in the parks. It was late afternoon, and we were starting out again after a prolonged stop for lunch and playtime for the children.

Heading west on Highway 2 snatches of a hymn were running through my head.

> God will take care of you,
> Through all the day.
> O'er all the way,
> God will take care of you,
> He will take care of you.

I mentioned the song to my husband, and we sang it a couple of times, and reflected how, on the previous day, God had taken care of our family and friends during a terrible thunderstorm, during the course of which we had become separated from our friends. Little did we realize how soon we would again experience that watch care.

Half an hour later, I was woken abruptly by the jerk of the car as my husband swerved to avoid colliding with an oncoming vehicle. Overcompensating, we went into a skid. The tent trailer we were pulling was out of control and hit the car on each side as we continued a zigzag pattern back and forth across the road. A tire on the trailer had blown, pulling us into the ditch.

As the trailer dug into the dirt and flipped, the car lifted into the air and rolled. When the car stopped rolling, there was absolute silence. I glanced at my husband, curled over the steering wheel, motionless.

"Am I the only one alive?" I wondered.

As if in response to my unspoken thought, I heard the click of a seatbelt and my oldest son, Zachary, said, "My seatbelts undone."

Nathaniel, three and a half years old, started to cry.

An unfamiliar voice spoke. "Everything will be fine. Don't worry."

I wanted to believe that calm, soothing voice. However, the words that followed were alarming.

"Don't move her. Wait for the ambulance," came another voice, bringing me to a fuller awareness of my position. I was hanging upside down, my feet resting on the shattered windshield, my seatbelt pressing hard into my hipbone. Panic set in.

"Will someone get me out of here?"

"I will," came the quiet voice of our friend Allan.

"Are you alright, Brenda? Doug, are you okay?"

My husband began to get his bearings as Ellen, Allan's wife, continued anxiously. "Your head is bleeding, Brenda. How do you feel?"

"Fine," I replied. "Please get me out of here."

Doug pulled out the camping knife that was strapped to his waist and tried to cut my seatbelt. It took some time because of the awkward position which he was lying in. Each jerk of the knife caused the belt to press tighter against my hipbone.

"Do you hurt anywhere, Brenda? Does your neck hurt?" Ellen kept checking.

"No, there's no pain," I responded, eyeing the pool of blood forming on the car ceiling just above my head. I was grateful for Ellen's experience as an ER nurse at a large hospital back home.

As the boys were released from their seatbelts, there were many hands to catch them so they wouldn't land on their heads. As soon as the boys were safely out, an ambulance arrived. My husband was cut out after a quick assessment by the EMTS. They took more time getting me out with very careful slow movements, as I was bleeding from my head.

I was laid on a board that was supposed to click together underneath me so that they did not have to lift me anymore than necessary until they could be sure of the severity of my head injury and have my back checked for injury. As they were checking my vital statistics, they were asking me questions to assess my brain function. I think I passed.

The state trooper had arrived and was getting statements from our friends and the rancher who had called in to report the accident. He was also checking tire tracks and the highway surface. When he was satisfied, he gave the nod for the EMTs to put me in the ambulance.

Unfortunately, the tall grasses in the ditch were getting caught between the teeth of the board, and just as they lifted me, the two sides of the board would disengage. After the second attempt, I offered to get up and walk to the ambulance.

"Sorry, ma'am, but you might have a head injury. We can't risk that."

Despite the seriousness of the situation, I could see the funny side.

The next attempt was successful, and we set off for the hospital. The EMTs continued to ask me questions, more detailed this time.

My sons and husband followed the ambulance into town in our friends' station wagon.

The doctor in Emergency checked me in and then called in an x-ray technician and a specialist. My sons arrived looking anxious. The state trooper took my husband away for questioning.

The doctor looked at my sons and asked them their names. When they replied, "Zachary and Nathaniel," he picked up the biblical reference.

"I suppose your parents are Mary and Joseph then. Yes?" he asked. Both boys laughed.

To keep them busy and take their minds off the situation, he looked at them and said, "What are you two boys doing standing there? This is a hospital and there's work to do. Nobody stands around in the hospital. Pick up those sheets and put them in the bin." He kept them scurrying around moving things, and soon they were relaxed and laughing.

X-rays were taken, and the specialist examined me. Both boys were checked and my husband as well, when the state trooper brought him back. Miraculously, I was the only one with injuries. The others all received a clean bill of health. I received stiches to my head and antibiotics for the injury to my knee.

As the afternoon drifted into early evening, there was discussion of what to do next. The doctor told us that the town we were in was celebrating their 100th anniversary the whole weekend. There were no hotel rooms or camping spaces available. He said that if nothing else came up, our family was welcome to stay at his place. He also offered our friends the use of his yard to park their RV.

As we were talking, a Baptist pastor arrived. He had heard of the accident and came to take all eight of us to his home. So many angels in that small town. God was certainly taking care of us through every day as the words of the hymn assured.

We stayed with the pastor and his family for two nights, reporting to our insurance company, filling out paperwork, gathering our belongings from the car, and arranging storage for the car and the trailer until all the decisions with the insurance were ironed out. It was made more complicated because of regulation differences between the two countries.

As we shared breakfast the next morning, the pastor's wife told us that they had been in a similar situation the previous year. They and their family had been traveling with friends in a van in British Columbia, Canada. A pastor there had taken in both families and helped them with all their arrangements. God was taking care of us in all ways.

The morning after the accident, I showed signs of delayed shock and the pastor's wife was able to identify what I was going through because of their experience. She helped me in so many ways, and most of the anxiety was settled with her loving and gentle counsel.

The second day we went through our belongings from the trailer and car, choosing only what we needed. All eight of us were travelling in our friends' station wagon. So, space was limited. We gave our food to our hosts, and they said that we could leave our camping things with them until we were able to return for them.

We left the following morning, arriving in Calgary by suppertime. The kids had enjoyed travelling with their friends. All eight of us stayed at my husband's parents' home. In the morning our friends left to continue their holiday, and we attended my sister's wedding. The wedding was held in a park on a beautiful July day, and once again, we were abundantly thankful for the multitude of ways God had taken care of us.

We were to discover when we arrived home three weeks later that a woman from our church had felt a heaviness on her heart on behalf of my husband. Even though she did not know exactly what to pray for that weekend, she had prayed, and the Holy Spirit had interceded on our behalf.

That afternoon in the emergency room, we were very aware of God's hand on our lives. Because of His constant care over us, there are no white crosses on Highway #2 for our family.

Joshua 1:9 says, *"Have I not commanded you? Be strong and courageous. Do not be terrified: do not be discouraged, for the Lord your God will be with you wherever you go."*

For the trip home, read "Just Get Us to Our Driveway."

Just Get Us to Our Driveway

We had been at my husband's parents' home for about a week. We still did not have a replacement vehicle after our accident in Montana. Our car was a write-off, and there were still ongoing questions about the tent trailer. Apparently, our insurance policy did not cover the cost of a temporary vehicle replacement. We were not financially able to purchase a new car until the accident claim was settled. We prayed each day, seeking guidance.

Isaiah 55:8, 9 says, "'For my thoughts are not your thoughts, neither are your ways my ways,' declares the Lord. 'As the heavens are higher than the earth, so are my ways higher than your ways and my thoughts than your thoughts.'"

We waited patiently for the Lord's thoughts to be revealed.

Well, I personally have not seen such an ugly, unkempt, beat-up vehicle before. My husband's brother brought it up to Calgary from Southern Alberta.

"It's not much to look at, but it should get you to Manitoba," my brother-in-law said.

I heard the word *should* echoing in my brain.

The men went out to the garage to tune up and check all the usual things. It didn't look any better, but it was the only available option.

"Really, Lord?"

Our thoughts were definitely nowhere near His thoughts!

The next morning, we loaded up the car and gingerly got in. We all prayed (a lot and fervently) and then set off. Friends from Manitoba and their three children had joined us and were travelling back with us. They were crunched in their vehicle. So, carpooling was not an option this time. Our friend's grin and the shake of his head brought the word *should* back into my mind.

We set off, and every time we stopped for gas or food, we all prayed together before getting back into the car. It was a good faith-building exercise.

We travelled to Regina the first day, stopping to stay at a hotel with a pool and waterslide. Five children had lots of energy to use up. The next morning, we went to the park by the river and ate our breakfast. Then we took the kids to where the ducks were. We had been there many times over the years as we travelled and had been introduced to feeding the ducks by my stepsister and her husband. The ducks and geese swarmed us. They were tourist-wise fowl!

More prayer and back into the vehicles to continue the journey home. The first few hours were uneventful. I am fine with uneventful. But the peace was not to last. The car started to miss a beat, as if struggling for breath, and the timing chain got looser and rattled louder and louder. So, we slowed down.

We pulled over to the shoulder of the highway, our friends following closely. The two men looked under the hood, discussing possible causes. They wiggled a few hoses and checked the radiator and the oil levels. We sat there for a while.

Finally, deciding that we should try again, we pulled back into traffic. Things seemed to be going fine. Just as we all relaxed, the car started rattling again. Pull over, check whatever we could think of, and resume our trip. That became the routine for the next several hours. Our pace became slower and slower.

When we stopped for lunch, we called to the Lord. This was our prayer: "Lord, thank you for being with us on this trip. Could you put Your hand on the timing chain and just get us into our driveway. We would appreciate that. It has been a long trip."

After a loud group "Amen!" we packed up the remnants from our picnic lunch and set off again. Each time the timing chain rattled, we slowed down and repeated the prayer—in both cars!

Finally arriving on the outskirts of Winnipeg, we gratefully set off on Ring Road. Our friends took their offramp, honking and waving. A few minutes later, we took our offramp.

Pulling into our driveway, we all breathed a quiet prayer of thanks. Before my husband could turn off the car, it took a long breath and quit. We all started laughing with delight at our answered prayer, that the Lord would get the car to our driveway. No amount of coaxing would get that car to start again. It was done.

We all loaded up our arms with bags and sweaters and toys to begin the trek into the house. As we entered the house, the phone was ringing. Our friend's daughter Melanie was calling to find out if the car had made it to our driveway. We assured her that it had and related to her parents that the car had truly died in the driveway.

A few weeks later, we were having a BBQ at the home of one of our parishioners. There were several families from our church. After the meal was over, they asked us to tell the story of our trip to Montana, the accident, and our eventful trip home. When we had finished telling the tale, there was quiet. The silence was broken with one man's enthusiastic response, "Can we go with you on holidays next year? You guys have adventures!"

Laid Down Bone

I had just received a surprise diagnosis. The doctor in Emergency had ordered an x-ray as part of the protocol of my late-night visit. He brought the x-ray into the examination room to show me and gave me the news. I had osteoarthritis in my neck. I was stunned, as the reason for my visit to Emergency was totally unrelated to my neck. I had no idea what osteoarthritis was. I had never heard of it.

He offered no further counsel, only adding that it was just for my information. Then we addressed the issue that had brought me there that evening.

More than twenty years have passed since I was diagnosed with rheumatoid arthritis and put on medication. I learned to manage my RA thanks to the advice of one of my cousins who suffered from a very aggressive form of the same condition.

I lost strength in my hands, and almost four inches in height. There were odd bone projections in my fingers but no swelling, and my left-hand lost bone mass. Additionally, both thumb joints lost bone.

After many tests and physio appointments, I was referred to a spine clinic in a large city three hours' drive from our home. After extensive tests and scans, the specialist informed me that there were several areas in my cervical spine that had missing bone. And that's when the diagnosis of osteoarthritis was reiterated.

The specialist waited to fuse my spine, but I declined. I didn't want to walk like a robot or have my driving privileges taken away. After some more discussion, he agreed to wait for one year. If there was no change or further loss of bone, I would have the surgery. My family, friends, and Bible study group prayed that I would not have to undergo surgery.

One year to the day, I was booked into the spine clinic. As soon as I arrived, I was sent down for an MRI. By the time I got to the specialist's office, the results of the MRI were on his computer. He showed me the MRI from the previous year and the MRI from that morning. There was a substantial difference. On the newest MRI, there was now bone where there had been only dark spaces the previous year. I was so excited when he said, "Brenda, you have laid down bone!"

I literally went home on a cloud, praising and thanking the Lord. My friends probably tired of hearing me proclaiming, "I laid down bone!" repeatedly over the next few weeks. The story doesn't end here. It gets better.

I continued to have problems with osteoarthritis, and it began to impact my life in very real ways. I was unable to unlock the seatbelt harness of my granddaughter's car seat and prayed as panic swept over me. Each time I was finally able to release the lock, or someone who I knew would appear and help me.

Pain in my neck and spine continued to plague me. One evening there was a prayer and healing service in our church. I sat firmly in my seat, resisting the urge of the Holy Spirit. My husband started to whisper in my ear, "You should go up."

I decided that neither of them was going to give up. So, I moved forward to join the line and waited my turn. I was anointed with oil, hands were laid on me, and prayers were spoken over me. When I was walking back to my seat,

I felt taller in stature, lighter in spirit, and was filled with certainty that I had been healed. I was certain that everyone could see the difference in me as I walked back to my chair because I felt like a new creation, a whole new person.

I went to my doctor and asked for tests to be done to confirm what had happened. When the test results came in, my doctor confirmed that I had no markers of osteoarthritis!

I have claimed the promises in Isaiah 58:11: "And the Lord will guide you continually, and Satisfy your desire with good things, and make your bones strong; and you shall be like a watered garden, like a spring of water, whose waters fail not."

Once again, the Lord heard our prayers and listened as only He can—in abundance, overflowing our cup, replacing mourning with joy.

Mira, the Miracle Baby

Our youngest son, Nathaniel, married his lovely Nicole. We were thrilled. Our first daughter-in-law! A few short weeks after the wedding, Nicole had surgery for cervical cancer. Two months later, we found out that we were going to become grandparents. We were ecstatic.

The cancer specialist was not ecstatic. He told Nathaniel and Nicole that she would not be able to carry the pregnancy to term. If they had realized that she was pregnant at the time, they would not have undertaken the surgery.

Nathaniel refused to accept the doctor's prognosis. "No, I claim this baby in the name of Jesus," he said. "The baby will live."

When they found out that they were having a baby girl, they chose a name, Mira Faith. Mira for *miracle* because she had been claimed in His name for protection. Faith because they had faith that God was able to protect this baby during the months of pregnancy.

Isn't this a great story of faith and confidence? Doesn't it make the hairs on your arm stand up? The story isn't over. When Mira was born, another miracle occurred. Mira was born with a full head of dark hair and with the umbilical cord around her neck.

The doctors and nurses assured Nicole and Nathaniel that this was not an unusual occurrence. When the cord was removed from Mira's neck, there were two knots in the cord. The doctors and nurses were amazed. One knot in an umbilical cord is cause for concern. Two is cause for extreme concern. Nathaniel and Nicole were informed that it was a miracle that Mira had survived the birth. Usually, two knots meant that the baby would have died or would suffer brain damage.

Nathaniel and Nicole had many medical staff peek in to see "the miracle baby" after the birth. At two-years-old, Mira had to show her nana how the TV remote worked. And she continues to teach me new things. Any time I don't know how to make my technology work, she has it all fixed in just a few minutes.

The Lord is an amazing God!

Be Careful What You Pray For!

My husband and I were living in west central Alberta. Our only granddaughter was living with her parents in Southern Alberta. It was just over a six-hour drive away, but it seemed so much farther.

"Lord, I would like to be closer to Mira, to spend more time with her, to establish a better relationship. She is so young that she barely remembers us between visits."

We were going down for Mira's second birthday party in the middle of October. Several days before our departure, we received a phone call from our daughter-in-law. She was six months pregnant and had injured her back. She was on painkillers and needed some help. Her mom had stayed home with her and Mira but needed to go back to work. We decided to leave our home earlier than planned.

We would be staying with my husband's father in Calgary and commuting north to Airdrie each day. Fortunately, we had been down in Airdrie just a few weeks before this trip. So, Mira had a vague memory of us, and it didn't take long for her to warm up to us.

First on the agenda was to help Tracy, Nicole's mom, put Mira's birthday party together. Tracy cleaned and picked up fruit and veggie trays and other food. Doug and I went to pick up the pre-ordered birthday cake, and I got to pick a party dress for Mira. It was very exciting but also took me a little longer than it should have. The stores were much larger than at home and the selection overwhelmed me. So, I came up with the ideal solution: I bought her two, one for the birthday party and another one for Christmas!

Then Tracy and I arranged party trays, sliced a variety of deli meats and cheeses, filled bowls with crackers and chips, and added two delicious dips that Tracy had prepared. I was getting tired, and the party had not even started!

The party was very busy and exciting. Mira and her cousin Jackson had fun playing with all the wrapping paper and, occasionally, some of the new toys. After the cleanup, we returned to Calgary and dropped into bed exhausted.

Monday was a day of learning Mira's routines and running up and down stairs to help Nicole and taking Mira for a walk. It was beautiful sunny weather for mid-October. Mira loved to look at rocks, grass, and every other little thing that we as adults miss because we are so busy getting somewhere else and we miss all the wonders around us. It was lovely seeing the world around us from the perspective of a two-year-old.

On one of our walks, our pathway went behind a string of houses. A dog tore out the patio door of one of the houses and stood on the other side of the chain link fence from us. The dog barked continuously and loudly. Mira stopped and surveyed the dog for a few minutes. She placed her tiny finger on her lips and made a "shh" sound very quietly. Watching the little girl so intently "chiding" the dog brought smiles to both my husband and me.

On Tuesday we packed up a few clothes for ourselves, and when we arrived at our son and daughter-in-law's home, we started to load our car with all the things that Tracy had packed for Mira. My husband was scheduled for lens replacement in his right eye, and we had to travel to Edmonton.

We were staying with our oldest son and his wife in Edmonton. Mira had not seen her aunt and uncle for some time. So, she was uncertain about them. In her world that meant she did not want to be hugged or approached by either Zachary or Christine. This was hard on both of them, as they loved children. Gradually they were able to gain her confidence.

Zachary had a few days off. So, he offered to take his dad to the hospital for the procedure. This was a relief, as I was uncertain how Mira would manage the long wait at the hospital. She'd had a lot of changes in the past few days. Mira and I passed the day in the apartment watching her favorite cartoons, reading, running in the hallway, and having a nap.

When Doug and Zachary finally arrived back at the apartment in the late afternoon, Doug lay down on the futon and quickly fell asleep. While Doug was in day surgery, Zachary had met with a lady who had purchased an old library catalogue file from me via Kijiji.

Mira watched her grandfather sleeping on the futon and quickly left the room. She returned with her little red coat and covered Papa up so he wouldn't get cold.

Zachary, Christine, Mira, and I went out for supper. I had forgotten what taking a two-year-old to a restaurant was like. Wow! Another good reason to have children while you're young!

The next morning Zachary took his father to an early morning checkup, and when he returned, we returned to Airdrie. Mira and her mom were happily reunited.

The whole process repeated itself five days later, when we had to return to Edmonton for the second lens replacement. This time though, Mira was very happy to see her uncle Zachary and took his hand and chattered to him as they went up to the apartment.

This time Zachary was working. So, I had to get Mira ready and pack a bag of snacks, drinks, and toys to get her through a long stay at the hospital. We arrived at the hospital and checked Doug in. Mira and I were directed to the waiting area. The waiting area was a very long hallway with seats on both sides. As I was walking down the hall looking for a place to sit, I spied a friend of mine from our home church. My friend was in the city for the day, as she had accompanied a lady who was also booked for day surgery. What a blessing!

Kathy pulled a few items from her bag and offered them to Mira. Novelty, a great thing for children and their busy minds. Between my bag and Kathy's bag, we kept Mira occupied for a few hours and had a good visit. Then Kathy's friend was released, and they left to return home. They had a three-hour drive. I was sad to see Kathy leave but very grateful for her help.

A few minutes later, I looked up, and walking in front of me was a retired man, also from our home church! I called his name, and he came over with a smile and sat down beside me. We chatted for a few minutes (he was also in for the day, accompanying an acquaintance having day surgery), and then Bill suggested we go to the cafeteria and have some lunch.

Just as we finished our lunch, a nurse walked through, asking for me. She explained that Doug was ready to leave, but he was still under the influence of the drugs he had received. She also gave me the prescription for the drops that we would need to pick up at a pharmacy on the way home. She reminded me that Doug had an early morning appointment the following morning.

Then she said the most amazing thing: "Your husband told us that you have night blindness and will have difficulty getting him to his appointment. The doctor and other staff discussed the problem, and we have switched Doug's appointment to a later time and to the other doctor's office, which is closer to where you are staying. Would that be okay with you?"

I was so relieved that I almost hugged the nurse. I was concerned about the appointment the following morning. My husband was not allowed to drive for a few more weeks. So, it was all left to me.

I gestured to my granddaughter and asked if I could have a wheelchair to get my husband to the car. The nurse said that she would bring Doug to me in a wheelchair a few minutes later. When I saw him, I was even more grateful. To say that Doug was loopy was an understatement.

He wanted something to eat. So, I got him a sandwich and a drink. As he ate, he repeated things over and over. He kept trying to get out of the chair. I had visions of him lying in a heap on the floor and me unsuccessfully trying to get him up.

Bill had been watching carefully. He said, "Would you like me to push his chair to the door for you so you can take care of Mira?"

I thanked him and went back to the waiting area to retrieve my bag and our coats.

By the time we were at the front door of the hospital, Bill had sized up the situation: a loopy husband in a wheelchair, a two-year-old who needed to be held onto, several bags of toys and snacks, a handbag, and a frazzled wife and grandmother. Bill suggested that I go get the car and bring it up to the door and he would wait with Doug.

For a reason that totally escapes me, the car was on the far side of the parking lot. It took quite a while to walk with a curious two-year-old, laden down with bags and books. Finally, Mira was installed in her car seat, and we pulled up to the front door of the hospital. Bill said he was just about to send out a posse to find us. It took the two of us to maneuver Doug into the front seat. I thanked Bill profusely. I don't know how I would have managed without his help.

Next stop, the pharmacy. I was not sure how I was going to manage the two of them in the pharmacy. So, I asked God to put Mira to sleep, not really believing that it was going to happen, as her mom had told me that she did not sleep in the car. Recent experience had borne out this fact.

When we arrived at the pharmacy, Doug insisted that he go into the pharmacy with me. As he could barely stand up straight, I was insistent that he not accompany me. Glancing into the back seat, to my surprise, Mira was sound asleep! I told Doug that he would have to stay with Mira while I went to fill the prescription. Not that I felt he was the most responsible person to leave a small child with, but there were no other options. I locked the car doors and took the keys with me. I didn't want to chance anyone getting out or trying to drive away. I was very grateful my daughter-in-law would never find out about my desperate decision. I could barely justify it to myself, never mind to a pregnant mother!

The pharmacist told me it would be a fifteen-minute wait for the prescription. As I pondered that information, I had a mental picture of me trying to support a loopy husband and hang onto an active little girl as I walked through a large Safeway all the way to the back where the pharmacy was situated and then wait for fifteen minutes. The picture made me laugh out loud. The pharmacy staff gave me funny looks. So, I decided to go check on my passengers. Both were sound asleep.

I looked over to my right, and there, at the other end of the strip mall, was a Starbucks. I ran towards it, happily imagining the comfort of a tea latte. Ah, just the smell made me happy! As I sped back to the pharmacy, I noticed that everybody was still sleeping. I ran back to the pharmacist, where, thankfully, the prescription was ready. It had only been ten minutes.

Just as I eased myself into the car, Doug stirred, and Mira woke up. Perfect timing. We headed back to the apartment, where Doug and Mira each went down for a nap, and I enjoyed my tea with a book and my feet up.

Early the next morning, we (meaning I, as Doug was not allowed to lift anything, drive, or bend forward) rushed Mira through her morning routine and finished packing and loading the car. We arrived late for our appointment, but the doctor was gracious about it. As he examined Doug's eye, I was unobtrusively trying to keep Mira from touching all the shiny objects and pilfering the papers on the doctor's desk.

Finally, we were on our way back to Airdrie. As soon as we hit the city limits of Edmonton, we were in big trouble. The highway was a sheet of ice. Traffic was moving slowly, and there were trucks and cars in the ditches in many places during that agonizing trip. I was white knuckling the steering wheel, Doug was moaning from the pain in his eye, and Mira was very fussy. Her morning had been rushed, and she was stuck in the car again.

When she dropped her toys there was no one to retrieve them. I had to concentrate on the road, and Doug could not turn around or bend down to search on the floor for the lost book or toy. I would periodically offer her a snack or drink, but she was not having any of that. I tried to talk to her reassuringly and calmly, but I doubt she heard me over her fussing. As I was not even able to give her eye contact, it was hard for a little one.

We stopped at Red Deer for a brief stop for lunch and then got back into the car. The trip which usually took just under three hours stretched out to four and a half hours. After lunch Mira again fell asleep. I was so delighted. When she woke up an hour later, she was able to drink her juice and play contentedly until we arrived at her home. To Mira's delight, not only was Mom there but also her dad, who had arrived home as well. Our son worked out of town. So, it was a special delight for Mira to find him home.

We were in Airdrie until the beginning of the following month, helping Nicole and looking after Mira. It was a delight to have that opportunity to get to know Mira better. I learned that God does indeed know our limits and He sends others to help us when we are at the end of our resources. He provides everything we need just when we require it. I learned how to winter drive on the highway, something that I was very fearful of. I no longer was afraid and felt stronger because I had faced my fears. Doug was not able to drive for three weeks. So, my skills were honed. I learned that I have more patience than I thought I had.

The other obstacle that I had to face was the three cats that my son and his wife owned. I'm allergic to animals, particularly cats. I was at the house for ten hours a day until Nicole's mom, Tracy, arrived home from work. The cats were kept on the lower level of the house while I was there. Some days I'm not sure who was more excited when Tracy arrived home, me or the cats. God stood in the gap for me, and I did not have any asthma attacks as a result of the cats' presence in the house. I was using a lot of extra medication, but that had never prevented me from having an attack at other times.

When we arrived back from Edmonton the second time, it was decided that Doug would not be able to stay at Nicole's house, as his eyes were extremely sensitive. Our son drove him into Calgary, and he stayed at his dad's house. I could not stay at Nicole's either, as there wasn't room. So, my niece, who also lived in Airdrie, kindly took me in for a week. I am unable to drive in the dark. So, I was unable to travel back and forth in the morning and evening to Calgary. Doug was able to rest and recover at his dad's as he was away at his timeshare condo in British Columbia.

"And we know that in all things God works for the good of those who love him, who have been called according to His purpose" (Romans 8:28 NIV).

Tracy and I worked together to make life work for Mira and Nicole. I would arrive by 7:00 a.m., and Tracy would leave for work after letting me know how things had gone the previous evening, what she had done, and what needed to be done. I would do the same thing around 5:00 pm., when Tracy arrived home. We shared housework, bathing Mira, and meals. Tracy would frequently pick up things we needed on the way home. It was such a blessing working together.

Most families don't get to know the other side of the family so well when their children marry. We were put together frequently, and I am always so thankful for Tracy's graciousness towards us and her family when we come to town. Tracy and I have decorated and prepared food for many birthdays and showers in the past three years, and I am sure that we will do so for many more festive occasions.

I also want to thank the Lord for our other daughter-in-law, Christine. Her family also includes us and treats us kindly when we are in Edmonton or when Zachary and Christine come to visit in Hinton. Christine's parents live in the same community as we do. It is a small world filled with many good things.

"Praise the Lord, O my soul, and forget not all His benefits…" (Psalms 103:2 NIV).

A Perfect Garden

It was the only year that I have ever had a perfect flower garden. I was so angry that the weeds didn't have a hope of survival.

Non-Hodgkin's lymphoma. It changed our lives. My oldest son was a month from his twenty-third birthday when we received the diagnosis. This diagnosis marked a pivot point for our family. Our lives had been turned upside down, but we determined to live with as much normalcy as was possible.

Zachary had to move back home, as he was not going to be able to work for the next thirteen months of treatment. Our home needed some renovations for this to take place. The dining room was divided in half so we could create a bedroom for Zachary. His previous bedroom downstairs had been converted into an office for my husband. The entire lower level of the house had been turned over to my husband's therapy practice. Space was limited. The same friends who had helped us renovate the basement to set up the business reappeared to help us build a bedroom upstairs.

We had the most amazing family, friends, church, and community. They gathered around us, supported us, prayed for us, visited, and called frequently. My mother always said that after she spoke to Zachary on the phone, *she* felt better.

Zachary's friends were fantastic. The first week after he was diagnosed, his male friends had dinner together every night with him. The young women left baked cookies outside his apartment door. Their support never wavered through the thirteen months of treatment. While they acknowledged his situation, they never treated him as if he were different. Several months after he was diagnosed, they planned a winter weekend in the nearby mountains. It was scheduled on a week that he didn't have a chemo. Still, he had his face washed with snow and had to pull KP duty the same as everyone else.

Many of the group worked shifts. So, they had different times free during the week. When he wasn't recovering from a chemo session, they would invite him out for a coffee or lunch, maintaining contact with as much normalcy as possible.

When Zachary started his treatment, I would accompany him to the hospital and sit with him for the three hours. But soon I had to return to work and could only drop him off. It didn't work out too well that first day. I was so restless that the principal of my school told me to go to the hospital and take the day off.

I looked at him uncertainly, "Are you sure? I asked. I was out the door before he finished saying yes.

When I arrived at the cancer center, all the patients were discussing their favorite foods, most of which, they could no longer enjoy. It was somehow reassuring that they could engage in such everyday conversation with such abandon and enjoyment.

I had always thought I would never be able to cope if anyone in my family was diagnosed with cancer, and it never entered my mind that it would be one of my children. But it's true that when the time comes, you are extended the grace you need to get through each day, sometimes if only for one minute at a time.

We have many happy memories of that year as well. It sounds rather bizarre to say, but it is true. It's because of all the people who stood with us, many of whom we had never met. Friends who were travelling in Europe told everyone they met about Zachary and asked for prayer for him and our family. Our younger son spent that summer in Thailand working at an orphanage. He met a group of young people who were there from Toronto, and they prayed for Zachary.

My sister, a single parent who had not been on a holiday for years, came with her youngest son from B.C. and spent ten days with us. My oldest brother took time out of his holiday to come and surprise Zachary with a visit. Every church in our town prayed for our family, even those who didn't know us personally.

The pharmacist found funding for us, as Zachary needed shots of Neupogen before each treatment, as his white blood cell count was too low to have treatment without it. When it was time for Zachary's first treatment, the funding had not been confirmed. I went to our pharmacy to explain to our pharmacist that I was unable to pick up the drug, as the funding had not arrived, but Merv just smiled and handed me the prescription and said not to worry. It was being taken care of.

Zachary had to have doses of the Neupogen each day for four days before his treatment could be given. I had to go to the hospital and learn how to inject the drug at home. Sometimes normalcy was hard to maintain.

We had a family reunion in Southern Alberta a few weeks after Zachary started treatment. My extended family is Norwegian and very reserved in expressing emotion, but they showed their caring in so many ways that weekend.

Our family doctor, Ross Dunbar, was very empathetic. He would call with news or information the first several weeks and would talk to all of us, not just Zachary. He knew this was impacting us as a family. Eventually, as we got over the shock, he only had to communicate with Zachary.

Our care group provided the funds to purchase a supplementary treatment plan for Zachary. It built up his immune system. The doctors at the Cross Cancer Institute told us that a strong support system as well as supplementary treatments all contributed to the successful treatment of cancer. I was very appreciative of their open attitude.

Several months into the treatment, Zachary was admitted to the hospital. He had managed to pick up a flu bug. So, he had to be isolated. When we went to visit him, we had to wear masks and gloves and wrap ourselves in gowns.

That week, a family friend went to visit him in the hospital. Steve gave Zachary a gift, an older diesel truck. It was a monster and took up a large portion of Zachary's meager finances. But it put a smile on his face. He loved that old beast. Steve also gave Zachary another gift that day. He gave him hope, something to look forward to.

Zachary had his struggles with depression that year. His friends and peers were moving ahead with education, careers, and weddings. The rest of our family was at school and work. He spent many hours alone at home. But the combination of prayer, friends, family, and his sense of humor all contributed to a successful outcome.

He affectionately called the ladies in the lab "the vampires" as they took blood before each session. He joked with the doctors when they asked how he was doing. He responded with, "I hear there are rumours that I have cancer," and then would laugh.

Not a day passed that either my husband or I would have taken our son's place if we had been able to. Not a day goes by now when we are not aware of how blessed we are that Zachary is a survivor of cancer.

Yes, my flower garden was initially weed-free because I was angry. I was trying to root out the cancer from my son's body. Later, the time spent with my flowers was a way to retreat from the reality of living with cancer. It was a time to enjoy the beautiful colors and smells, the order of nature. It was a time to pray and talk with the Lord, to draw comfort in His strength.

Hold On

That Sunday was an amazing day. My partner in the children's ministry and I were in the church kitchen. We were discussing how we were going to present the Bible story in the large group session later that morning. A little four-year-old boy ran into the kitchen. He stopped in front of us, his eyes shining.

"Can you guess what I did today?" he asked.

"What did you do?" I responded.

"I praised Jesus today!"

"That must have made Jesus so happy!" I gave him a big hug as he nodded in agreement.

We looked up to see his mom standing on the other side of the open window above the serving counter. Her eyes filled with tears. She confirmed that Owen had accepted Jesus into his heart that very morning. We all rejoiced at this good news and praised the Lord that a new child had been added to the family of God.

Owen and his mom left to share the good news with others. As we turned around, there was a lady waiting to talk to us. "I want to bless you ladies today," she said, rummaging around in the bag she was carrying. Then she handed us each a little plaque which blessed our work as teachers. We were so pleased with our gifts, thanking and hugging her.

Later that evening was our Annual General Meeting for the church. What an incredible meeting it was! The expanded leadership team presenting their reports were upbeat and passionate about the ministry of our congregation. We reflected on the previous year's AGM. We had been not able to meet our budget and were faced with cuts in funding to all programs. Now, a short year later, we were talking about our increasing need for space, the increased attendance, and our upcoming Capital Funds Drive as we sought God's face about a move to larger facilities, either through building or buying an existing building.

After the meeting was over, the pastor and I were speaking, and he affirmed the work that my partner and I were doing with the children's ministry and how it had contributed to the growth of the church. I floated home on a cloud of peace and blessings that evening.

I had been reading studying and writing about peace for the previous few weeks. As I'd read about peace, I had felt increasingly peaceful and felt that I had learned to understand and practice peace in a new way.

There is an old saying, "Keep your eyes on God and your ear on Satan." Satan was not going to leave me in peace. He was not happy that I had learned to trust God more deeply. Satan wanted to destroy my confidence that I could rest in God's presence and in His peace in all circumstances.

The next evening, Satan launched his attack. We received a voicemail telling us our youngest granddaughter, not quite two months old, was in the hospital. They were doing some tests, and the doctor's believed she had a rare bowel condition. They needed to do a biopsy to confirm their diagnosis.

It's amazing how effectively and completely my sense of peace was rocked. I didn't lose my sense of peace, but it was wobbly. I fell asleep that night after my husband and I had prayed. I woke three hours later, and my brain kicked into gear. I battled fear, helplessness, and worry about our little Jericho. I questioned the Lord about allowing a tiny baby to face such a crisis. I prayed about the terrible anxiety that her parents were experiencing. I prayed for her older sister and the upset in her life that she was too young to understand. After several hours I was spent and just lay there in my bed.

I was quiet. God spoke to my heart, using precious promises from His Word.

"Trust in the Lord with all your heart and lean not on your own understanding; in all your ways acknowledge him, and he will make your paths straight" (Proverbs 3:5,6 NIV).

"Be joyful always; pray continually; give thanks in all circumstances, for this is God's will for you" (1 Thessalonians 5:16-18 NIV).

"Do not be anxious about anything but in everything, by prayer and petition, with thanksgiving, present your requests to God. And the peace of God, which transcends all understanding, will guard your hearts and minds in Christ Jesus" (Philippians 4: 6,7 NIV).

I slept peacefully.

The Piano

We had a beautiful solid oak upright grand piano! It was old and had a lovely tone. When we moved to Winnipeg, Manitoba, it took five men to move it into our living room. Did I mention that it was heavy?

Later that evening, when we were alone with our piles of boxes, my husband said, "When we move again our ad will say, 'House for sale. Includes piano.'"

Our oldest son had started his lessons on that piano when he was five. It always held a place of pride in the living room, wherever we were living. It was a beautiful old instrument and held many memories. Our youngest son was an adventurous boy. He was the one who wanted to reach for the sky. Literally.

One day I was baking in the kitchen and heard some unusual noises. When I called, it became very quiet, an ominous sign as any parent knows. I flew into the living room and there was my preschooler standing precariously on the lid of the keyboard reaching for the top of the piano! He grinned at me, excited that he had almost reached his goal. When my heartbeat returned to a more normal pattern, I lifted him down, explaining the danger of his actions. He just looked at me and said, "Up high," and grinned again. It was not the last of his climbing adventures.

We lived in that house for several years, and when the time came to move, we did not advertise, "House for sale. Piano included." I was so relieved, but only for a short time. My husband insisted that the piano be sold. He was returning to graduate school. We would have to move for him to attend school and then again when he was finished.

I was heartbroken to let the piano go, but there was no choice. I advertised the piano, mostly by word of mouth, hoping that no one would want it.

A lady from our congregation called me, saying that a friend of hers was looking for a piano for her daughter. Could she come and see it? I reluctantly agreed. She bought the piano, and before I could draw my next breath, the piano was being rolled out the door by professional movers.

As it turned out, my husband had made a wise decision. Over the next seventeen months, we moved five times, spanning three provinces. But I never forgot the piano.

About a year after we had finally settled down in one place, I received a call from one of my aunts. She was selling her house and moving to another community. She was uncertain what to do with the pump organ that she owned. She was wondering if we were interested in having it. We were delighted and made arrangements to move it from Saskatchewan to Northern Alberta. The organ arrived two days after Christmas. What a memorable day!

Our youngest son started lessons on the organ, and we had music again in our home.

Many years passed, and many moves happened. One afternoon the lady from our former congregation called me. We had kept in touch with Christmas cards over the years. She asked if we remembered the lady who had bought our piano so many years before. The lady wanted to start downsizing and was wondering if we would be interested in having our piano back. I think that I almost stopped breathing. Joyce gave me Marg's phone number so that I could contact her.

I called both of my sons to tell them of the possibility. To my surprise, they both told me that they had never forgotten the piano either and were ecstatic that we could have the piano again. I then called Marg in Winnipeg. I could not believe that she remembered us.

We spoke for a time, and she concluded the conversation this way: "I am not selling you the piano. I am giving it to you. I have always felt that the piano was very special to your family."

I was overwhelmed. This woman had heard the whisper of God in her ear and had followed that whisper to our hearts. I will be forever grateful for this woman's willingness to be a messenger of God's blessing and promise to give us the desires of our hearts.

God saw the misery of his people in Egypt and promised he would take them to a land flowing with milk and honey (Exodus 3:7, 8). He always keeps His promises for He is the same yesterday, today, and tomorrow (Hebrew 13:8). He saw we were sore in spirit with the loss of our piano and wanted to take us out of our misery.The honey of this promise fulfilled filled my mouth with sweetness.

I have pictures of the boys when they were small with the piano, and now I have pictures of them playing the piano as adults. These pictures remind me of God's goodness and are sweet drops of honey to taste and savor.

Angels Unaware

I had just finished a busy afternoon at one of the community schools in which I served, providing Speech and Language Therapy. After loading my therapy bag into the trunk, I jumped into the car and started it. Glancing around and making sure there were no children near my car, I eased out of my space.

Very quickly I realized that my vehicle was not in reverse. It was in Drive, and I had just driven the front end of my car up over the concrete barrier and had pushed a section of the fencing in front of the barrier down onto the sidewalk.

In shock, I had the sense to turn off the ignition. Opening the door, I got out and looked at my front end. The front end was suspended with the tires hanging over the other side of the concrete barrier. I knew enough not to back up the car. I didn't want to wreck the undercarriage.

I returned to the school to report the fence damage to the principal. When I had related what had happened, she burst out laughing. My efforts to make her understand the seriousness of the damage to the school property only caused her to laugh louder.

I called my husband between clients and asked him to meet me at the school when he was done for the day. When he arrived, he and I tried to lift the car up and then hoped that the car would roll back off the barrier. That didn't work.

We were pondering calling for a tow truck when a white truck with business decals stopped behind my car. Two men in white painter's t shirts and pants got out and asked if they could help. They went to the front of the car and assessed the situation. Then they asked Doug to put the car in Neutral and put on the brake once they got the car up and over the concrete barrier. In less than five minutes, they had grasped the front fenders and lifted the car up and off.

Then they looked at the damaged fence lying on the sidewalk, lifted it, and reconnected the pipes at the top. Good as new! You couldn't tell there had been any damage. We were standing with our mouths hanging open and examining the front of the car. As we turned around to thank the men, they were gone. We looked up and down both streets, but there wasn't even the sound of a retreating truck.

We took our car to the local garage for an estimate of the damage and the cost or repairing it. The mechanic called an hour later. One tire rim had been bent. We couldn't believe it.

Later, Doug recalled the business decals on the truck. He told me that someone from that company lived across the street. He remembered seeing the truck from our kitchen window.

After looking up a phone number, he called and described how we had been helped and wanted to pass along our thanks. The man who answered the phone told Doug that there was no one fitting our description of the men and informed us that there were never two men in any of their trucks.

Did I mention that both men had shoulder length snowy white hair? And did I mention that we never saw that truck across the street from our house again?

And Then there Were Ten

We had settled into our new normal. My husband and I were retired and were creating a home that included our son and his two daughters, aged two and four. Our son worked away from our community on a rotating schedule of two weeks away and two weeks at home.

In the middle of one of his rotations away, he called us with a request. Friends of his needed a place for themselves and their three children to stay. They were travelling from a nearby province and were coming to a community near us. A family member was in hospice care and was nearing the end of his battle with cancer.

"Could they stay with us?" my son wanted to know. With our family of five and the friend's family of five, there would be ten people in our home.

To be honest, I was a little overwhelmed by the request, so asked for the day to work out the logistics. Later that night, at our weekly care group, I asked for prayer. The ladies asked how they could help. I had figured out beds for everyone except the little girl.

One couple volunteered a small pink plastic bed that was exactly the right size for the preschooler. I called my son back later that night and said we could offer hospitality to his friends. I still was a bit worried, wondering if I could manage everything, but I knew we wanted to help this young couple.

We set up a cot and the pink bed in the family room for two of the visiting children. My son's room was prepared for the couple and their baby son. Our son used a foam mattress on the floor of my study. My granddaughters, my husband, and I were in our own beds.

Our visitors arrived, and it was a busy time. Five children, four of whom were under the age of four, one three-month-old baby, and five adults. Mornings were early, and breakfasts were chaotic. The three little girls would create pictures on the easel with markers and chalk while breakfast was being prepared. Then the visitors would leave after breakfast and return in the afternoon.

It was early spring. So, all the kids could play outside in our large backyard. As I was preparing supper, Derick and Riley would take all the kids outside to our backyard to play. Derrick was very creative and invented games and activities to keep the kids occupied.

Suppers were also chaotic but fun. Baths and bed were next. Prayers and stories completed the kids' day. The adults had fun visiting and playing games in the evenings, accompanied by the gurgles of little Moss, the youngest of our "family of ten." We played one game that required throwing dice. So, we put a towel on the table. We did not want to waken the sleeping children.

So many memories were created during the following two weeks!

My granddaughters and Zao, the little girl who was visiting, were good friends and spent many hours dressing up and playing make believe in the girls' room as only little girls can. There were several princesses, loaded down with jewels dancing around the house, as well as dragons and monsters stomping around.

One day stands out in my memories of this time. I couldn't get any water from the kitchen faucet, but water was leaking under the sink. My husband, Doug, and son Nathaniel worked on it for about an hour but were unable to fix it. They called my father-in-law, a retired plumber. He couldn't really understand what the problem was without seeing the pipes. Doug went into the city to get him and returned one and a half hours later. Soon, we had three grown men taking turns lying on the floor and wrestling with the faucet above.

Our extended family arrived home shortly after, and Haye, aged nine, was sent up to the bathroom to get water whenever the men needed to pour some water down the sink.

It was soon time to begin prepping supper. As I set up the frying pan on the kitchen counter right next to the plumbing trio, four young helpers surrounded my work area. Derrick decided that I was going to need some help with my eager "assistants." So, he joined my team. Now we had nine bodies in close proximity working on two different projects. Did I mention that I had decided to try a brand-new recipe that evening?

In spite of the close quarters, and the noise and potential for accidents, no one was injured, supper turned out delicious, and it was deemed that the faucet needed to be replaced. There were eleven for dinner. It was chaotic but great.

Tucked in among all the activity were the lessons I learned. I prayed every day for stamina for all the tasks that needed to be completed and God graciously answered those prayers.

As Derick and Riley joined Derrick's family each day, it was hard for them. All the family members were people of faith, but each of the parents had children who needed to be taken care of.

I saw such grace in Derrick and Riley and later, in Derrick's parents, whom we met for the first time after their son passed away. I was humbled in the face of their grace and strength under the difficult circumstances.

I was also blessed as I watched Derrick and Riley care for their children and gently discipline them when necessary. I saw the grace they extended to each other and to all the children in our home. We had known Derrick and Riley for a number of years but were very impressed as we got to know them better.

God brings many blessings as we are willing to help His other children, even when we are uncertain of our ability to do so.

The Plumber

My husband leaned down to put the salad spinner in the lower cupboard. A minute later he exclaimed, "What's this?"

I looked over and Doug was hastily pulling things off the bottom shelf. A pile was accumulating on the floor.

"Look," he said, pointing to the cleared shelf. "Water."

"I'll grab a cloth and you can wipe it off," I offered helpfully.

"No, the entire shelf is covered with water. I think we have a leak."

Doug then pulled open the next cabinet door under the sink. Water there too. Doug also found water on the pipes.

We swung into emergency mode. Doug pulled everything off the upper shelf in the first cabinet. I started to move utensils, bowls, and other kitchen paraphernalia from the cabinet onto the counters and table. I sent my granddaughters down to the laundry room for my supply of rags, and we set to mopping up.

I looked at my full dishwasher of dirty dishes and the pile of more dirty dishes stacked on the counter. I sighed. I had forgotten to run the dishwasher earlier. So, now the problem with the pipes was a really big deal.

After we had cleared up the water, Doug set to checking the pipes and hoses more closely. His groans and exclamations did not auger any good. As I helped the girls through their nighttime routines, I heard Doug running up and down stairs, checking pipes and connections. After the girls were settled for the night, Doug and I sat down to pray and realized that we needed some guidance and most likely a plumber.

God is good. We had two people who would give us good counsel. The first was Doug's father. He had been a plumber before his retirement. As the conversation progressed, it focussed on one or two possible causes and solutions. Next, Doug called a friend who had built his own home and was very capable and a good thinker.

Lyle came over, and he and Doug examined all the pipes and connections and possible solutions. He told Doug that he didn't have the right tools, but he was able to recommend a plumber in town.

When Lyle mentioned the plumber's name, I mentally slapped my head. The plumber was married to our church secretary, whom I knew quite well. I had known her husband was a plumber but had forgotten.

Doug called Geoff, and he arranged to come over the next day. He was quite busy but promised he would come later in the day. Meanwhile, the dishes were continuing to pile up. I had handwashed all the accumulating piles on the counter, but that was my limit.

To our surprise, Geoff showed up early the next day. Geoff looked over the pipes and listened to Doug's explanation of how we found the leak. Then Geoff set to work. He solved the problem and then mentioned that there were several pipes and hoses that were unnecessary and not being used and asked for permission to remove them. When he was finished, I had more storage space in the two lower cabinets. However, the Lord was not finished helping us yet.

As Geoff was packing up to leave, Doug asked him if he had experience installing boilers. The reply was in the affirmative. He looked at what we had and outlined how and what he would do. It was simple and clear. We were so excited.

Having two other companies in and explain what was needed had left our heads spinning. We had no concept of what they were going to do or why. Both Doug and I had hesitated to sign a contract, as we'd both felt a check in our spirits. But we knew Geoff could be trusted. Plus, he took the time to be clear about our options and answer our questions.

We believe that the pipe problems under the sink were God's way of leading us to His provision of the right plumber for the boiler installation. Once again, He provided what we needed at the right time and with the right person. I smiled contentedly as I turned on my dishwasher.

The next day, as we were preparing breakfast, my oldest granddaughter commented, "It is sure nice to open the drawer and see all those knifes and spoons!" Another blessing.

"Bless the Lord, O my soul, and forget not all His benefits" (Psalms 103:2 RSV).

Broken Pipes

I was teaching a Tuesday morning Bible study at my church. Most of the ladies were young moms with a sprinkling of women like me who had finished raising their children. As well as sharing what we had learned during the week while doing our homework in the current study, we had a time of praying and sharing.

We had been unable to sell the home we had in our previous community and now owned another home, where we had decided to retire. I asked the ladies to pray for the sale of our former home. Having two mortgages when entering retirement was never part of our plan. One morning I was sharing with the group that we had received news from our renter that water was coming into the basement and there was very low water pressure.

We had called a plumber to check out the situation. He said the pipes had broken, but they weren't sure if the broken pipes were on our property or farther along, past our property line. If the break was past the property line, the town was responsible for the repairs. Otherwise, we were responsible. The town arrived, did an exploration, and confirmed that the problem was not on town property.

Our tenant had a friend who could dig up the lawn and identify the exact location for us. Sadly, the break was on our property. There were several large trees, and the roots had grown around the pipes and had eventually put so much pressure on them that they had burst.

We had to call in a specialized company that had the equipment to dig up our basement floor, then dig the lawn up to access the roots and the broken pipes, dig up the roots, and replace the pipes all the way back to the house. The estimated cost was $10,000. We were stunned. We didn't have the money, but the repairs had to be done, and we had a responsibility to our tenants.

Our Bible study group had been praying for the sale of the house, and now were adding a prayer to find the money for the repairs. Our tenants moved out while we tried to find a solution to our problem. Finally, after many weeks of prayer and discussions with the company that was prepared to take on the job, they offered us the option to pay the bill in three separate payments. This was kind of them to try and help us out, but we had two mortgages and were already stretched to our limit.

As I shared the option with my ladies, it was very quiet around the table. Then the silence was broken. One of the older women did not agree that this was a good solution and demanded to know where the verse in the Bible was that we were using as the answer. I didn't have a specific verse at the time, but it seemed to be the only open door.

Later, as I was eating lunch, my telephone rang. The call was from one of the ladies in our church. She said she and her husband had ben talking and praying for the previous few weeks and had decided that they would like to pay the bill for the repairs.

I just about choked on my food. I was so surprised. I had never even met this lady's husband. Neither had I met anyone who had $10,000 to give away!

I double checked that she had said they intended to cover the bill. I was sure they were offering us a loan. She assured me they were gifting us this money to pay the bill. They only asked that we not reveal their name to anyone. They wished to remain anonymous.

The next morning, during my devotions, I was praising God for the way He had provided for us, and my eye fell on this verse: *"We know that in everything God works for good with those who love him, who are called according to his purpose" (Romans 8:28 RSV).*

I had my verse and would often see this verse being played out in my life at other times. He is a good, good God, and He loves His children.

We met soon afterward and arranged for the transfer of the money. We made plans with the company to begin the work, and a few weeks later, we had new pipes and a new lawn—and our tenants could move back in.

The Week of Blessings

The day had finally arrived. We were returning to the community where we had lived for nineteen years. It was time to sell our home. We never dreamt selling the house would take five years.

We'd had a couple of tenants, and the house was desperately in need of repairs before we could put it on the market. Repairs, replacements, and renos were on our list.

We packed the back seat and the box of our truck. Paint cans, brushes, drop cloths, putty knives, and ladders were collected and packed. Drills, screws, nails, and hammers followed. Next came food, spices, pots, frying pans, tea and coffee, jugs, kitchen tools, soap for the dishwasher as well as dish soap, sugar, cream, milk, and cookies. Soil, fertilizer, and grass seed were piled in the back of the truck box. Bedding, warm clothes, towels, phone chargers, books, personal items, all the paraphernalia of life. When the truck had only room left for us, we stopped and hoped we hadn't forgotten anything essential.

We had a six to seven-hour drive and were grateful for the bare roads. It was late April, but we were returning to a community that was close to the Rocky Mountains. So, we were prepared with warm sweaters, jackets, and boots.

Arriving in the mountains, we set about unloading, unpacking, and setting up our temporary home. Our realtors had lent us a table and some chairs. We bought a floor lamp for the dining room. Friends had dropped off pillows and blankets, dishes and cutlery, and someone even dropped off a coffeepot. We were ready to begin our adventure.

Later that evening, my husband's brother Rob and his wife, Marilyn, arrived and set up their little private corner of the house and, of course, more tools. After they were finished, Rob started patching the walls so we could start painting first thing in the morning. Marilyn had brought freshly baked cookies and muffins as well as ingredients for evening meals.

The next morning, we were joined by Lyle, a good friend from the community we had moved to, as well as Dave, a dear friend from our years spent in this mountain community.

Naturally, they each brought more tools. My living room floor was a forest of paint stir sticks, toolboxes, power tools, screwdrivers, painting supplies, hammers, and ladders. The paint cans were lined up like soldiers ready for orders.

Soon, the house was filled with the sound of paint cans popping open, ladders being set up, and drop cloths being spread like blankets over the floors.

While the men were deciding where they would start, Marilyn and I were cleaning up the kitchen and loading the dishwasher. I was very grateful that the dishwasher was still in good repair. We planned our main meals and checked that we had all the ingredients and equipment needed.. Then it was time to serve coffee. Our hungry crew really appreciated the cookies and muffins.

At lunchtime Dave left to take care of their new puppy and take his lunch break. He returned later that afternoon and worked until suppertime. This was his schedule for the entire week.

After supper it was apparent that one thing was missing. Dessert! I suggested a trip to the local Dairy Queen. My suggestion was unanimously accepted.

Tuesday morning arrived with more help. Our oldest son and his wife were in the community, staying with Zachary's in-laws for a few days. Zachary and his wife had some time booked off from work and had arrived the evening before. What a blessing to see them! They arrived early in the morning and introductions were made. They agreed to do the outside work.

We had left the yard in a park-like condition and were saddened to see the weeds where flowers had bloomed and the ATV tracks where lush grass had grown. I can still see Zachary and Christine out in the cool spring day, with watery sunlight, pulling weeds, cutting back bushes, and hauling debris away from the flower beds. When I asked if they were cold, they said, "Not at all." The heavy labor warmed them right up!

Zachary and Christine spent the morning clearing out the flowerbeds that were surrounding the house. After lunch they spread new soil where grass had been then seeded and fertilized. They watered the large area that they had covered before they left. We were sad to see them go but so grateful for their help. They felt bad that they didn't have time to make the flowerbed on the east side, but we told them that they had done so much already to add to our week of blessings. They really worked very hard, and we realized that there would not have been time to get it done if they hadn't been there.

The days were busy, but quickly a routine was set. Lyle had brought music to accompany our labors. The music set a peaceful atmosphere as the men painted, repaired, and did renovations. Marilyn and I cooked, cleaned, served meals and coffee, and were gofers each day, as the men found they needed specific nails or screws or tools. It would have been impossible to anticipate some of the things that were small but necessary.

The staff at the local Home Hardware store would spot us coming through the doors and ask, "What do you need?" Sometimes, while we were at the store filling the list the guys had given us, my phone would ring and more things were added to our list.

Marilyn and I also went to the grocery each morning to find something to accompany coffee twice a day. Working men need lots of fuel, especially sweet things apparently. But each of them asked me not to tell their wives about the sugar laden sweets. I just smiled. Guilty pleasures.

One morning as Marilyn and I walked into the local grocery store, the scent of fresh baking assailed our senses. We followed our noses. We scored hot fresh sugar doughnuts for morning coffee. The crew showed their appreciation, barely touching their coffee until the last sugary crumb was gone.

I would never have made it without Marilyn. She and Rob had volunteered to come and help us, and this was an enormous blessing.

On Tuesday my good friend Lois appeared at the door, ready to join the crew for the day. She cleaned the carpet in what had been my husband's office. Then she scrubbed the utility room, walls, floors, and four appliances.

As I was visiting with Lois late in the afternoon, working alongside her, Lyle came into the utility room. After some general chat, Lyle asked me if I was planning on taking the refrigerator back home with us. When I told him that we had no need for another fridge, he asked if he could have it. I said, "Yes, of course." Then he looked over at the small chest freezer. He asked if we were taking it back with us. I said we couldn't, as our truck was full.

"I have room in my truck," Lyle said. "How about I take it home for you?"

I was overwhelmed once again. I had wanted to take the freezer with us when we moved out five years previously but was unable to. Deferred answers to prayer are extra sweet.

Blessings poured over us each day, engorging our hearts with gratitude to our heavenly Father. We were humbled that so many joined with us in these labors, giving unstintingly of their time and talents.

Wednesday morning brought another addition to our crew. When Lyle had arrived on Monday, he announced that, on Wednesday, Kim was coming. I searched my memory bank. Was Kim his son-in-law's name? I couldn't remember but didn't think so. The way Lyle had announced Kim's coming made me feel as if I should know who he was. I was reluctant to ask for fear of offending Lyle. So, like Mary, the mother of Jesus, I was left to ponder this in my heart.

Wednesday the front doorbell rang at 9:00 am. Squeezing past a ladder, I opened the door. A tall bald man stood there smiling.

"Is this house the one where there's lots of painting going on?" he inquired.

"Yes," I responded with a smile. "You must be Kim!" I invited him in. Within minutes he joined the other guys and fit in as if he had been with us all week.

Kim left that evening as he had to head into the nearest large city to attend a funeral the next morning. He left, refusing our offer of something to eat, as he had a three-hour drive ahead of him. Kim left but never will we forget the blessing of his time with us.

By this time, the men had developed a routine of work. They assessed the work that needed to be done each morning, divided up the chores, and spread around the house. After lunch they would return to their labors, at which time they would switch areas. You could hear quiet conversations going on throughout the house. By moving around, they visited each of the others at some point. Lyle was the one who worked mainly on the repairs needed. He had great skills and was a born problem solver. The front hall closet door was hanging on by a screw or two, and we had assumed that it would need to be replaced. Blinds were damaged, and we also assumed they would need to be replaced. The costs were adding up, but Lyle quietly checked out these areas and asked Doug and I to meet with him. He told us he was pretty sure we could find the materials needed for repair instead of replacement.

Then we went into the second bedroom, where the mirrored closet doors were missing. The tenant had removed the doors, as his daughter had nightmares and was certain there were monsters hiding in the closet. It took us a while to find the missing doors, but when we did, we were delighted to find them in good repair. They were moved upstairs and stood outside by the shed. After lunch they were to be reinstalled.

Just as we were finishing lunch, there was a loud crash! Jumping up, we ran outside only to find the closet doors lying on the grass, shards of glass everywhere. We all stood around the shattered remains of our closet doors dumbfounded. I searched my mind to see how this was a blessing. I finally decided that at least no one was injured. In fact, the entire week was injury free, and we were very grateful to God for His protection!

Thursday morning brought our youngest son to the house. He had been away working in the northern part of the province and was at the end of his shift, so decided to come to join our work party. He brought the remainder of his groceries to add to our fridge. Marilyn and I laughed as we opened his food box. There, on the top of the pile, were some peppers. We definitely had an abundance of peppers, as Marilyn and I had both included some in our loads. They added flavor and color to our spaghetti sauce and veggie plates.

Later Thursday Lyle invited Doug and I down to the family room for another consultation. In the family room was a large gap in the Gyprock. We had covered it with a mirror, but it needed to be fixed. Lyle said he could put another piece of Gyprock in the gap and blend it in. We happily accepted his offer. When he was finished later that evening, we regarded the wall in awe. He had blended it seamlessly. The entire room looked better as a result of his work.

Our next-door neighbors Ron and Gail were eager to see the changes we were making. They were eager to see the end of the tenants but sad that we were not going to return. Every time we had trouble with our tenants, Ron would tease us that it was a sign we should come back.

We managed several quick visits over the week with Ron and Gail. They were making plans to move within the next couple of years and had bought a home in another province. When I heard their news, I told them that if they weren't living next door, we wouldn't be returning.

Ron and Gail were such good neighbors and friends, and we missed them especially. We would often get together for a game of Skip-Bo. It was amazing, one might even say suspicious, that when we played pairs, the guys always won. They were such a blessing to us when we lived in the house. Many years, many memories.

Friday Lyle was heading back home. After breakfast there was a bustle of packing his tools and other belongings. The guys all helped move the fridge upstairs and onto the truck. Then they loaded the small chest freezer into the truck. After prayer we waved goodbye and then returned to the day's work.

Dave had taken on the job of sanding the exterior dining room windows, prepping them to be stained. The windows were ajar, and he could get in on the conversation with the others, who were painting the dining room walls.

We had decided to have an Open House on Friday evening and invited Ron and Gail, our realtors, and several friends to come and see the difference that all our efforts had produced. We received many compliments on the new paint colors and repairs and changes that had taken place thanks to so many talented friends and family members who had gathered around us and helped us get the house ready for sale.

Each day we prayed together before starting our day, and many others who couldn't be with us were praying on our behalf. We were tired but very grateful for all those who gave unstintingly of their time and talents.

We were injury-free this week and were reminded once again of the good friends we had left behind, of our new friends that we had made in our new community, and above all, of the many blessings that God had rained down on us this past week.

We lived the reality of Ecclesiastes 4:9, *"Two are better than one, because they have a great reward for their toil."*

Saturday dawned and we got a shock when we looked out the window. A winter storm had blown in during the night. Snow was piled up in drifts everywhere. It was very windy, and we could see that the road in front of the house was covered with ice.

We checked the road reports, as Rob and Marilyn were planning on leaving that day to visit their son and his family, a three-hour drive away with good road conditions. We urged them to wait, but they decided they would leave as planned. Over the next several hours, they texted back the conditions of the road. The news was very bad. It took them two hours to get to the next town, a trip that would normally take forty-five minutes.

Nathaniel, Doug, and I debated the wisdom of following them, but as our son said, "We'd be fighting every mile we drove, and it could take us up to ten hours or more. We'd be exhausted, assuming we could even get home tonight."

As soon as we made the decision to stay for another day, I called my best friend, Mary-Jean, Dave's wife.

She promptly invited us to stay at their home for the night. I immediately agreed. A real bed sounded delicious after a week sleeping on hardwood floors. Nathaniel would get another night to visit his friends.

Mary-Jean and I might even get some time for shopping after we returned all our borrowed household things. And cleaned up the house. And packed. By the time the truck was loaded with everything but the food, it was late afternoon. I called Mary-Jean to let her know we were on our way to her house, and we mournfully agreed that it was too late and too cold to go shopping.

Arriving at their house we joyfully greeted the dogs and Dave and Mary-Jean. They had spread out a feast of appetizers and drinks. We hadn't stopped for lunch, so fell on the feast as if we were half starved. After a wonderful supper and lots of visiting, we all curled up with popcorn and bowls of ice cream in front of the TV.

The next morning, we had another shock. Bright sunshine poured through the windows. We checked the road reports, and the news was much better. After one of Dave's signature breakfasts, we prepared to leave. It was very hard because it still felt like home.

We met Nathaniel at our house and packed up the food from the fridge and headed for home. The sun stayed with us most of the day, and the roads were bare all the way home. The snow was piled high on each side of the highway and spread like blankets over the fields as far as we could see. The icing on the cake of a week of blessings. God is so good!

There is one more blessing that happened at the very end of the week. Find it in the story "The Yellow Door."

The Yellow Door

It was almost the end of the week. Soon it would be time to list our home for sale. As my sister-in-law Marilyn and I were cleaning up the bathroom, I glanced out the window. Across the street and down about five houses, my eyes were drawn to one of the neighbor's homes.

"Look," I said to Marilyn. "That house has a yellow door. That is just the color of door I want. I wonder what the paint color number is?"

"The only way to find out is to go and ask," she replied.

I was reluctant to do this, as I was fairly sure they were new owners. I hadn't lived in my house for five years, but I knew the previous owners, and they would not have painted their front door yellow.

Soon I found myself, notebook in hand, reluctantly being escorted down the street by Marilyn to the house with the yellow front door. I should have remembered that Marilyn was a woman of action.

"What am I going to say to say? I feel silly." This was my final protest as Marilyn rang the doorbell.

The door opened and Marilyn grinned at me.

"Hello, my name is Brenda, and I'm the owner of the house on the corner."

The lady smiled and nodded. "Hi, Brenda."

As I was pondering whether she agreed that was my name or that I owned the house on the corner, she told us her name was Sarah. I had a vague feeling she seemed familiar, but I couldn't place her.

I complimented her on the door color and the welcoming arrangement of baskets on her front step. She invited us into her home, and then I explained why we had appeared at her door.

I asked if she remembered the paint color number. She did and said it could be purchased at the local Home Hardware store. She assured me it was still available. She knew this because she was the store manager.

My skin was beginning to tingle. I said the only problem was that we were leaving to return to our home several hours away two days later and would not be able to get the doors painted before we left.

I asked her if she could give me the name of the person who had painted her door. She smiled at me. "I painted my door." My heart started to race. "Would you be willing to paint my two doors?" I asked her.

"Yes, I would," she replied.

She explained the process and gave me an estimate of the time required. She invited us to come to the store the following morning, as she was working that day, to pick up the paint and the tools required for the job.

I was so happy. I was also curious. The feeling had been growing within me that I had met Sarah before. When I mentioned this to her, she agreed that I, too, seemed familiar to her. It took us awhile to go over places we could have met. Finally, I told her where I had worked when I lived there.

Her face cleared. "I think you did the speech therapy for my youngest son. "

She told me his name, and we realized that was how we knew each other. We were so pleased and amazed we had figured it out.

Her son was a preschooler at the time he was seeing me, but was now seventeen years old. Just at that moment, the door opened and her son walked in.

I looked at the lanky teenager and smiled. "It's been a while," I said, and we all burst out laughing.

The next morning Marilyn and I arrived at Home Hardware. I ordered the paint and added the tools that Sarah needed for the job, paid for them, and thanked Sarah once again for being willing to undertake this job.

She did a great job, sending me pictures as the project progressed.

I do not believe this meeting with Sarah was merely a coincidence. I believe God superintended every step.

In the RSV, Romans 8:28 says, *"We know that in everything God works for good with those who love him, who are called according to his purpose."*

I do not believe in coincidence. God is a God of order. He has a plan and a purpose for each of us.

The Best Laid Plans

I sighed as I finally gave in to reality. All the planning and dreaming of celebrations for our 50th anniversary came to a full stop. Our plans and dreams were confronted with the reality of the coronavirus pandemic.

The trip to New York in the last week of November would have included evenings filled with live theater, daily trips to the museums, and walking tours of the Big Apple. The second trip would have included driving along the Eastern Seaboard of the U.S., being dazzled by the changing colors of the trees, and visiting flea markets and antique shows.

Just a few weeks before our anniversary, we were overwhelmed with the second wave of the pandemic. Poof! We were now not able to assemble a celebration, as we were being asked to restrict our associations to the people who lived in our home.

With the numbers of COVID-positive results and related deaths, we no longer felt comfortable having dinner at our favorite restaurant. So, we moved to plan C. This necessitated a change of our paradigm. From very busy and filled with new and amazing experiences, we moved to low-key and familiar.

When we woke up, our son surprised us with coffee for my husband and tea for me from our favorite barista. The three of us sat and chatted while listening to the first of eleven new CDs we had ordered with love songs from the 50s and 60s. Our goal was to listen to the entire collection that day. It was a great start to our special day.

(Our son's presence caused us to remember that he was also present at our 13th anniversary. He was three weeks old. His older brother was in school. So, the three of us went out for a celebratory lunch. We received a lot of attention with a newborn at our table. It was a fun and relaxing lunch.)

My husband and I went out for the afternoon, snacking and visiting some favorite places around the nearby city, where we had lived as kids and young adults. Both of my sisters called, and we had long lovely conversations. They had been the bridesmaids at our wedding. When we arrived home later, we saw a delivery truck pulling away from the front of our house. We had received a lovely edible fruit bouquet.

Our son had prepared a wonderful supper of our favorite foods, adding stuffed mushroom cups, one of our favorites. It was a great evening, as we shared some of our favorite memories of previous anniversaries and continued listening to our CDs.

Nathaniel was our official anniversary photographer for the evening. One picture that he took was of us in a chair in our living room. The chair had been given to us by our eldest son on our 25th anniversary.

At 11:00 pm we watched a sappy movie. (There are always dozens of Christmas romances on at that time of year). We crawled into bed about 1:30 am. It wasn't as easy to get up in the morning for church as when we were twenty-somethings, but we'd had a very happy anniversary day. After church on Sunday, we drove to the church we had been married in. Nathaniel took outside pictures of us in front of the church that I had grown up in, while unaware the congregation inside sang the hymns of my childhood.

Low-key and familiar worked to make a memorable and happy time!

Oh! And we did listen to all eleven discs in our music collection.

Mole Surgery

My husband, Doug, was looking in the mirror one morning. "Look at these bags under my eye. I don't want to look like this," he complained. I was surprised. Doug had never mentioned his physical appearance before. He was a man who had always been very comfortable in his skin.

After several weeks of complaining, he decided to consult our family doctor. When he returned from his appointment, he was very unhappy.

"The doctor said it was just a sign of aging and I should get used to it," he informed me glumly. Doug did not agree with the doctor's opinion. He kept asking for another opinion. After several visits, the doctor finally gave in. He referred Doug to an optometrist in our town. He wrote something on a prescription pad and told Doug that he could go straight over to the optometrist's office and he would be seen.

Dr. Cowie had spent some time working with an eye specialist in the city, and she examined Doug and agreed with him that the bags under his right eye had nothing to do with aging. She referred him to an eye specialist, Dr. K, in a nearby city.

We discovered that a visit to this new office required a very long wait in the waiting room. The doctor finally examined Doug and said he felt Doug needed surgery. Another referral was made. Surgery was scheduled. The surgery was a complete success, and the surgeon was very happy with the healing process at the post-op appointment.

About ten days later, the surgeon's office called to tell us that Doug was being referred to yet another specialist, a mole surgeon. We were bewildered, and after some discussion, it turned out that they had sent a piece of the skin from Doug's lower eyelid for a biopsy. The biopsy showed he had mole cancer, a skin cancer.

Before we met the mole cancer surgeon, Dr. C., Doug had to go to a dermatologist to determine if he had the cancer on any other part of his upper body, as this type of cancer was usually found in areas most often exposed to the sun. The dermatologist found signs of cancer on Doug's upper body but assured us that they were benign. By this time, we were sending prayer requests out to family, friends, and our church.

At the pre-op appointment with the mole surgeon, Doug underwent more tests and exams. The doctor explained the procedures and said his office would call us when they had the surgery scheduled. They also explained that we would be spending the better part of the day at his premises when Doug came for the surgery. We weren't too worried because we knew that God was in this and would continue to walk with us through the surgery and whatever followed.

The day for surgery arrived. My friend Alice had travelled from a nearby province to stay with me for the day of surgery. I was very grateful for Alice's presence. Doug and I knew without a doubt that we were being prayed for that week. We had a peace that passed understanding.

For the entire week, we felt light in the Spirit and supernaturally calm. This had never ever happened before. So, we knew we were in the presence of God the Healer. We enjoyed each day as we waited. We were not touched by anxiety or worry. We had absolute confidence that God had our backs. We had many friends and family members who were praying.

I must confess that the day of the surgery was a very long day. We arrived early in the morning and waited in the waiting room until Doug was called to be prepped for the surgery. Alice and I were directed to another waiting room. We talked with some other families that were waiting for their loved ones. One lady was waiting for her husband and told us that her husband was there for his second surgery. She praised the skill and care they had received with Dr. C. during her husband's first surgery. Several others in the room also said they were very happy with previous surgeries their family member had undergone with Dr. C. The unsolicited affirmations were very comforting.

It was about noon when Doug appeared in the waiting room, his eye swathed in bandages. He was starving and wanted to go to the cafeteria to eat some lunch. I started to laugh. That was so typical of my husband, always ready for a meal.

Doug had to wait while the tissue removed from his lower eye lid was sent to the lab to determine if all the cancer had been removed. We had been told that, in some cases, they had to repeat the procedure two or three times before all the cancer was eradicated.

After a couple of hours, Doug was taken back into the surgery suite. We had waited for about thirty minutes when a nurse approached me. She said Doug was getting dressed and would soon join Alice and me. There was no need to repeat the procedure! We were so happy and started texting our many prayer warriors with the good news. After going over procedures for post-op, we left to return home.

Six weeks later we arrived at Dr. K's office. When he removed the bandages, we were shocked. Deep red and purple bruising covered most of his eye, making Doug appear to have been badly beaten.

The doctor smiled and said, "This looks very good. It's healing well."

For the next three years, Doug had to book checkups with Dr. C. and Dr. K. Each time they were pleased. There was no cancer!

Each time, we were pleased and continued to be grateful for God and His goodness and for the peace that we'd had as the surgery was upcoming.

"O give thanks to the Lord, for he is good; for his steadfast love endures forever!" (Psalms 107:1)

The Whisper

"You will need to take care of Doug."

This was whispered into my thoughts for a few weeks, sometimes more than once each day. These thoughts did not worry me but rather prepared me that something was going to happen. I was being mentally prepared for changes in our daily life.

We were in Edmonton visiting our oldest son and his wife for a few days. Arriving on a Saturday evening, the four of us went out for supper at a Boston Pizza. We had a very enjoyable evening eating and catching up on each other's news and making plans for the next day.

At breakfast the next morning, we realized our plans had to change, as the weather was too cold to be outdoors. After breakfast we scattered to get ready to leave the house. Doug went outside to warm up our SUV. the rest of us finished our preparations for the day.

I heard my daughter-in-law Christine yell, "Brenda, come downstairs right now!"

Just as I reached the bottom step, Christine said, "Doug fell."

I looked around the living room, searching for my husband. Christine's words didn't make any sense. Doug wasn't anywhere in sight.

"He fell outside."

Just then there was a knock at the front door. My son Zachary and a young man I didn't know were holding up my husband between them. After settling Doug on the couch, another young man, who was on the phone with the EMT dispatch, asked my daughter-in-law for her cell number so dispatch could continue the conversation with a family member.

Christine handed her phone to Zachary, who was asking Doug questions to determine his cognitive ability. The dispatcher was listening to Doug's attempts to respond. He told my son that an assessor would soon arrive to assess Doug, as well as the firemen and the ambulance. He assured Zachary that he would remain on the phone until all the emergency personnel arrived at the house.

Doug, who had been unconscious when the neighbor found him, kept slipping back into unconsciousness. He needed to remain conscious until the emergency crew arrived.

People began to arrive, and soon we had ten people in the living room. Once the assessor had completed his examination, most of the emergency people left. Only the EMTs were still with us.

As Doug was prepared to be put into the ambulance, the EMTs were on the phone with dispatch finding out which hospital to transport my husband to. They were going to take him to University Hospital, where my son worked.

Zachary, Christine, and I followed in the car, stopping only to pick up some tea for me. Arriving at the hospital, I was the only one allowed to enter. Zachary and Christine left, asking me to keep in touch via text. I spotted Doug immediately and went to his side. He was still on the ambulance gurney, surrounded by the two EMTs. We all went into a side room, where they found a chair for me. They asked more questions about his medical history and were very kind and concerned about how I was doing.

Soon we were moved into a cubicle in Emergency, where Doug was transferred onto the bed. As the EMTs waved goodbye, Doug's nurse came in and introduced himself to Doug and me, and then took my husband's vitals.

He found me a chair and asked if I would like some water. I pointed to my large bag, which was filled with water, tea, and books. I smiled. I was prepared. I had spent many hours in emergency rooms when my mother had been ill recently.

Soon the doctor arrived and asked many of the same questions we had already been asked several times. He directed the questions to Doug, but as Doug was unable to answer, the questions were directed to me. Doug had no memory of his fall and, to this day, has not remembered what happened.

After the doctor finished his examination and reminded me not to let Doug fall asleep, he said he had ordered a CT scan for my husband. I prepared for a long wait but was pleasantly surprised when an orderly arrived about fifteen minutes later to take Doug for the scan. And soon Doug was back in the room.

Time passed. I talked to Doug to prevent him from relapsing into sleep or unconsciousness. He would frequently ask, "What happened?" or "Where are we?" He was very puzzled and did not retain anything that I told him.

The doctor reappeared within about thirty minutes. He told us that Doug had a concussion, but there was no bleeding in the brain. I sent up a prayer of thanks. The doctor explained that the radiologist had to read the CT scan before Doug could be discharged from the hospital. In the meantime, the doctor had ordered an x-ray for Doug's right elbow. It was very painful. We think he hit it on a nearby fire hydrant when he fell. His elbow was massively swollen, and the bruising was deepening. I was very grateful that Doug had not hit his head on the fire hydrant, as it had many sharp edges.

Another orderly soon arrived to take Doug off for his x-ray and shortly returned Doug to me. We had now been in the hospital for four hours. Over the next hour, the doctor returned to tell Doug that the x-ray showed that nothing was broken in his elbow. Another piece of good news to be thankful for.

After the doctor left, Doug's nurse arrived, armed with pain meds, water, and ice packs. The nurse was a quiet, competent man. As he made Doug comfortable, we chatted. He had only been nursing for eight months, which was surprising because he was so sure of himself and had a great bedside manner. Each time he entered the room to check on Doug that day, he checked with me to see if there was anything I needed. He was such a gift.

Doug fell asleep, and I read my book, did a few crosswords, and occasionally walked around to stretch my legs. One time when I was standing outside of the cubicle, a passing nurse stopped and enquired, "Did someone not get you a chair dear?"

I assured her that I had a chair but needed to move around for a few minutes and stretch my legs. This happened each time I ventured out of the cubicle. The staff was so very kind.

The hours were beginning to feel very long. I reached for my notebook, deciding that I would journal the events of the day. My first sentence was indicative of how tired I was becoming. "We have been in Emerg for over six hours. I have run out of tea, water, and patience."

Time continued to pass slowly, even though I had lots to think about as I was journaling. As I paused at one point, I overheard some staff talking. They were saying that, as it was the weekend, only one radiologist was on duty for the entire hospital. I sighed. This explained the long wait but was not comforting news.

Eventually the doctor arrived. The radiologist had read Doug's CT scan. There was still no sign of bleeding in the brain, but he had written some additional information in his report. The doctor explained that Doug had a very bad concussion and suggested that we might want to consider Doug being admitted to the hospital.

I thought it was a good idea, but Doug flatly refused. After some more discussion, the doctor advised us to see our family doctor when we returned home. We thanked him and called our son to pick us up. On the way to our son's home, we had to stop the car a couple of times as Doug felt very nauseated and got sick. Once back at our son's home, Doug went to bed.

The next morning when I went downstairs for breakfast, I found that both of our sons had been very busy organizing how we were to get home.

The Ailing Washing Machine

We bought our current washing machine and dryer ten years ago. They served their purpose admirably, both for our tenants and our family of five plus our many guests.

The dryer went first. It stopped heating. We called an appliance repair technician that we found online. He arrived and assured us that the dryer was well built and was worth the cost to repair. I parted with a princely sum and breathed a sigh of relief. Perhaps too soon.

Six months later, the washing machine started making growly noises, which increased in ferocity each time we used it. We had to call a different repair technician this time, and he said there was no point in him coming as the bill would be higher than the cost of a new machine.

We started the search. Two things quickly became apparent: because this brand of machines was no longer manufactured, we had to choose another brand, and we were never going to find a matching color. Each day the search became more frustrating, and the laundry piled up.

We did find a washing machine with a good record of reliability, but by the time taxes, delivery charges, and the warranty were added, we were paying almost twice the cost of the machine itself, which was discouraging.

As the laundry piles continued to grow into mountains, I decided to pray over our machine. I asked God to keep the machine working without the ominous noises. I gingerly loaded the first pile of laundry into the machine and held my breath. No noise. It was healed!

I don't know how long the warranty for healed washing machines lasts, but I have washed dozens of loads since I prayed, and I'm grateful for every one of them.

Clearance

I was browsing on social media one morning and saw an ad for a system that would keep the leaves and seeds out of our gutters. The ad offered a free estimate. I was interested, as we had many trees on our property, and my husband did not enjoy clearing out the gutters, as he was afraid of heights.

After filling out the form provided, I submitted it. A few minutes later, my phone rang, and it was a rep from the eaves protection company. That was fast!

After a few questions, the rep set up an appointment for a salesman to come out, promising it would only take a few minutes. Brian and my husband hit it off immediately, and they went outside to assess what our needs were, chatting like two old friends.

Eventually, my husband returned to the house, saying that Brian was measuring. As promised, he had completed the job in just a few minutes, and the three of us sat at the dining room table. Brian explained the process and extolled the product. Then reality hit. The job was going to cost us almost $6000.

Although we were impressed with the product and knew that we needed the gutter guard, it was beyond our budget. Brian offered us several payment options, including having the work done that year and starting the payments the following year. We had to say no. If we didn't have the money at that point, we couldn't be sure we would have it the following year.

About a week later, as I was enjoying a supper with seven other ladies hosted by a good friend of Mine, my phone rang. Normally, I would decline a call during supper, but I had the urge to answer the phone. When I picked up, I didn't recognize the caller ID but still felt compelled to accept the call. To my surprise, it was Brian, the salesman from the gutter guard.

He told me his company had just finished a very large project and had some product left over. Brian's boss was debating returning the unused product to their distribution center two provinces away, which would be expensive. His boss decided he would offer the product at clearance prices instead. He asked Brian if he knew anyone who could use it. Brian went on to tell me that he thought of Doug and I right away. He had enjoyed our earlier visit and was excited to make this offer to us. When he checked our information, he realized the product on offer was the color we had chosen, and there was more than enough for our home.

I was in for another surprise. The cost was going to be way less than half the original price quoted and there would be no interest charged.

I told Brian I would discuss it with Doug but because I would be getting home late, it would be the next morning before I could get back to him. Brian said that would be fine.

Ten minutes later, my phone rang again. I sighed, annoyed that I had not turned off the ringer. It was my husband. I told him about the call with Brian. Doug said yes, we would accept the offer. So, I called Brian back and arranged to meet with him the following afternoon to sign the papers.

The ladies I was having supper with were very excited when I related what had happened, and we prayed for Brian. We all felt that it was a divine appointment.

As I was preparing for our meeting the next day, I was thinking about what we could do or say when Brian came for the meeting. The word that came to my mind was *food.*

I said, "Okay, Lord, but that might be tricky. This is supposed to be strictly a business meeting."

The meeting went very quickly, as Brian had already started the paperwork. In passing, he mentioned that he had skipped lunch, as his previous appointment had gone longer than expected. Immediately, the word *food* sprang back to my mind.

When we finished providing the information Brian needed, he sent all the paperwork in for approval. We now had to wait, but he assured us it would only take 10-15 minutes.

Doug offered Brian a cup of coffee and some banana bread that I had baked the previous afternoon. He was delighted.

As we were waiting, he commented how quickly and smoothly everything had gone. He smiled and said, "When things move like this, you have to know that there's something going on."

I agreed and replied, "We would call this a blessing."

Brian nodded. He went on to say he had heard of that through his Catholic upbringing.

As we said goodbye to Brian a few minutes later, I felt as if a good friend was leaving our home. I hope we meet Brian again.

Did you notice that we never asked God for the money to have this product installed or for a special deal on the product? We just accepted that it was beyond our budget. But God loves to shower His children with gifts, which makes them even sweeter.

God is such a good Father!

The Garage Sale

We had a commercial Keurig coffeemaker in our home, and we loved it. Once you have a commercial version of a Keurig, there is no going back to the size sold in stores. The water reservoir is large and seems to be bottomless. It works very well for entertaining and large groups.

Sadly, one day it died. My son went online to order a new one. He came to me with bad news. The price of a new one was very high and had increased by a substantial amount. Even my son could not agree to the purchase of a new one. I went into our storage space and retrieved my mother's one-cup coffeemaker. It took longer, as it had to be refilled frequently, but we still had our coffee and tea in the morning. Many times, I missed the convenience of the commercial Keurig but still appreciated that the money could be better spent in other places.

I love garage sales, flea markets, and estate sales. I don't have to buy anything. It's really about the hunt. I have many beautiful items around my house that I picked up over the years.

One Saturday my husband and I had been garage saling. We were ready to stop and head for home, as we hadn't found any treasures this time. As we turned a corner, I saw an open garage door. I pointed and said, "Lets go see. Just one more!" My husband pulled up at the open door and followed me into the garage.

There were two ladies in the garage, and I quickly apologised, saying that we would leave, as they were obviously starting to pack up. Graciously, they invited us to look around. We chatted as I glanced over a few items on the tables. The ladies told us that they were clearing out some things that had belonged to their mother before she died.

As I leaned over to look more closely at something on the table, my foot moved forward and stuck something. I looked under the table. There was a large box with "Keurig Coffeemaker" printed on it.

Pointing to it, I asked, "Is there a Keurig coffeemaker in that box?"

When they said it was, I asked to see it. My husband dragged it out from under the table. As he did, I realized how big the box really was. I asked if I could look at the coffeemaker. When the box was opened, I could see that the manufacturer's packing had not been touched. It was exactly like the one we had owned. I was very excited and asked the cost. I mentioned that it was a very reasonable asking price, but they didn't care, they just wanted it to be gone. We have used it to make many cups of coffee, tea, and hot chocolate, and I'm very thankful for each one of them.

Many people believe that we should not pray to God about "small things." They say He isn't interested, that He has more important things to do with His time. I don't agree. Remember the first story in this book, "The Little Red Book"? Some would say that was a small thing, but it taught me that God listens and that He cares. I have never forgotten those two lessons and those lessons became a foundation stone that my relationship with God and my faith in Him were built upon. I hadn't prayed about the Keurig, but God knows everything about us, and He likes to give us unexpected gifts.

Divine intervention comes in many ways.

Manufactured by Amazon.ca
Bolton, ON

35923549R00081